Things Shaken – Things Unshaken

Things Shaken – Things Unshaken

Reflections on Faith and Terror

Colin Morris

 EPWORTH

British Library Cataloguing in Publication data

A catalogue record for this book is available
from the British Library

0 7162 0610 2
9780 7162 0610 1

First published in 2006
by Epworth Press
4 John Wesley Road
Werrington
Peterborough PE4 6ZP

Typeset by Regent Typesetting, London
Printed and bound in Great Britain by
William Clowes Ltd, Beccles, Suffolk

Contents

Part Three – 24/7

Remembering Brian Duckworth

Introduction

I have never kept a diary, but because as a preacher and broad-caster I am required from time to time to comment on world affairs, after the attack on the Twin Towers in New York in 2001, I began to make some notes. I thought I might use them in *Thought for the Day* and in sermons on the general theme of 'Faith and Terror' – which looked as though it was going to be a huge issue for the foreseeable future. How momentous became clear when the coalition forces led by the United States and Britain invaded Iraq, starting a war whose legality is still being hotly contested, which sharply polarized public opinion in Britain, and inflamed Muslims throughout the world.

At a time when it is taken for granted how secular the West has become, Osama bin Laden triggered an old-fashioned religious war that pitted President Bush's Christianity against Al Qa'eda's radical Islam. Theology, which had been slumbering gently in the cloister and divinity school, was rudely awakened and found itself in the front line; the questions raised by the attack on the United States and its aftermath could not be understood without it. Standard works one had read long ago for examination purposes had to be dusted off – Augustine and 'Just War Theory', Luther pronouncing on tyranny and anarchy, and Reinhold Niebuhr writing on virtually any topic across the spectrum of what might loosely be called political theology.

Then what became known as the international war on terrorism took a new and frightening turn. The cult of death embodied in the suicide bomber, having spread from Israel to Iraq, turned up on our own doorstep; not in the form of insurgents invading this country from some Middle Eastern melting pot but as residents of the UK, some of them born and bred here. This appalling development caused ferment in the Muslim communities and made the whole society fearful as to what might happen next.

I am not an academic theologian; like many Christians I do my theology on the march, trying to keep my footing through the fire and whirlwind, battling to make sense of tumultuous events and listening through the din for the still, small voice of God. As a broadcaster I have the additional challenge of speaking not just to the community of faith but to society at large. These reflections are the result, and I have made no attempt to bring those which began as *Thoughts for the Day* up to date in the light of subsequent events. As a real prophet has said, 'What I have written, I have written.'

But this does raise an interesting issue about the nature of prophecy. Though there are rare men and women in the Church whom we describe as prophets because they see further and deeper than the rest of us, in fact all Christians are bidden to try their hand at the trade – Moses' wry wish, 'Would that all the Lord's people were prophets!' (Numbers 11.29) was answered at Pentecost where all present 'were filled with the Holy Spirit and began to speak' (Acts 2.4). From that moment on, prophecy ceased to be the monopoly of an elite and becomes an essential dimension in the witness of every Christian.

Of course, a cynic might echo the words of Horace Walpole, 'The wisest prophets make sure of events first!' as he observed how biblical criticism was beginning to make some Old Testament prophets seem like conjurors caught stuffing rabbits into hats when the theatre curtain rises prematurely.

Isaiah's prediction that the Jews would be freed from captivity during the reign of King Cyrus a hundred years later was highly impressive. Then probing scholars detected the work of a Second Isaiah interwoven with that of the First and writing as a contemporary of Cyrus. Daniel's colourful soothsayings become a little pallid when his book is re-dated to reveal him writing of past events and not future expectations. And so on and on.

What in fact modern biblical scholarship has done is to humanize the Old Testament prophets. No longer do they stand on the stage of history as mindless megaphones, booming infallible messages from a transmitting station beyond the stars. They were men of their time, immersed in events and occasionally magnificently wrong in their estimate of the drift of things. We revere them not for the infallibility of their judgements but for their perspicacity in tracing the elusive pattern of history, broken and enigmatic, and yet deriving meaning from God's sovereignty over it. No Bible translation panel would dream of rewriting the text of Isaiah and Daniel to bring their prophecies into line with the historical record. That is how things looked at a given moment to God-filled men and they spoke out because they could not remain silent.

Now I am not labouring under any delusion of grandeur in calling the Old Testament prophets in my defence. It is a truism of experimental science that we learn as much from our mistakes as our successes; to lay bare the mechanics of the train of thought by which we have reached contested conclusions about current events is useful to those coming after us who are theologically better equipped or armed with more information.

As to the structure of this book: I have succumbed to the popular habit of using ideograms for momentous dates – the day the bombers struck America, 11 September 2001, is now universally known as 9/11; the date of the London bombings on 7 July 2005 is already being spoken of as 7/7. So the first two parts of the book deal with these atrocities and their aftermath; then I have added a third section, 24/7 – an ideogram which denotes what is all round the clock, perpetually true – to deal with issues which I believe are enduring but still relevant to the Christian's worldly obedience at the present time.

I acknowledge specific quotations in the footnotes, but I am indebted to a number of books for general insights into the issues with which this book deals – Peter Singer's *The President of Good and Evil* (Granta, 2004), and *What I Heard about Iraq*, by Eliot Weinberger (Verso, 2005). I learned much about the thinking of Al Qa'eda from John Gray, *Al Qa'eda and what it means to be modern* (Faber and Faber, 2003); Sam Harris, *The End of Faith* (Free Press, 2005), and from a most illuminating article in the April 2004 edition of *Prospect* in which Bhikhu Parekh conjures up an imaginary dialogue between Mahatma Gandhi and Osama bin Laden. Oliver MacTernan's *Violence in God's Name* (Darton, Longman & Todd, 2003) is also essential reading. All biblical quotations are taken from the New Revised Standard Version, unless otherwise indicated. I am grateful to the BBC for permission to reproduce material that was originally broadcast.

Part One – 7/7

The Arithmetic of Horror

In the space of a few days our minds have been trying to cope with the arithmetic of horror. On Thursday over 50 people died in the London bombings, and 700 were injured. So far this week, 297 civilians and nine American soldiers have been killed in Iraq. To-morrow is the tenth anniversary of the slaughter by Serbian forces of 8,000 Muslims in Srebrenica; and the G8 Summit of Nations currently meeting at Balmoral has been told that 30,000 Africans die every day of starvation. Then on Sunday we commemorated the sixtieth anniversary of the end of the Second World War whose dead totalled an estimated 61 million.

It is worth pondering for a moment that awesome statistic. It includes 21 million Russians, 10 million Chinese, 7 million Germans, 6 million Poles, 2 million Japanese, 800,000 French, 500,000 Americans, and 400,000 Britons.

In one sense, these figures are mind-numbing; in another, they are meaningless. We cannot weigh in the balance London's dead against Baghdad's; Coventry against Dresden, Stalingrad against Tokyo. Any life is infinitely precious to someone, and if to no one else, then to God.

But 60 years on, we can draw some morals from that titanic struggle between the years 1939 and 1945 which left a mountain of dead. The simplest one is that evil did not win. This is not to say that the Second World War was a morally transparent clash between our side – the goodies, and their side – the baddies. Even when we believe the cause is righteous, our actions are tainted by the very evil we are trying to get rid of.

It was a close-run thing, but evil did not win. It had the technology, the brain-power, the absolute control over the lives of millions. The iron machines were thrown against frail human flesh. They smashed and twisted and blasted through remorselessly, but still didn't win. In the last resort, the sheer resilience of the human spirit withstood all the forces trying to crush it.

Commenting on this amazing human capacity to survive, the Italian-Jewish writer Primo Levi who was incarcerated in Auschwitz wrote, 'Precisely because Auschwitz is a great machine to reduce us to beasts, we must not become beasts. To survive, we must force ourselves to save at least the skeleton, the form of civilisation. We must walk erect, without dragging our feet, not in homage to camp discipline but to remain human.'[1]

He watched Jews march to the gas ovens with the words of the first commandment on their lips, 'Hear O Israel, the Lord your God, the Lord is One.' They had the alternative of cursing God and their identity or of dying with dignity. Stripped naked of all but their integrity, the overwhelming majority preserved it to the end.

Levi, a scientist who even under extreme conditions did not lose his powers of observation, then drew this conclusion:

Not only in the crucial moments of selection for the gas chambers but also in the grind of daily life, believers lived better. It was comparatively unimportant what their religious and political faith might be. Catholic and reformed priests, rabbis of the various orthodoxies, militant Zionists, naïve or sophisticated Marxists and Jehovah's Witnesses – all held in common the saving force of their faith. Their universe was vaster than ours, more comprehensible. They had a key and a point of leverage.[2]

---

1 Primo Levi, *If This Is a Man*, Abacus, 1960, p. 105.
2 Primo Levi, *The Drowned and the Saved*, Michael Joseph, 1988, p. 123.

That testimony was unsolicited because Levi had no intention of becoming a believer, and never did. A great writer, he suffered periodic depressions and finally took his own life in 1987. When he wrote of believers occupying 'a vaster universe' than non-believers, he presumably meant that in their different ways, they were committed to causes greater than themselves, which would survive their mortality.

I have a tattered press clipping which includes a photograph showing the philosopher Bertrand Russell, then in his late eighties, being marched off to gaol for protesting against nuclear weapons. Regardless of one's opinion about the issue itself, the interesting question is: why did he bother? Statistically, the chances that he would still be alive when someone pressed the red button to take the world off its hinges were remote. Why should a very old man want to endure the miseries of prison for an issue which was in a strict sense none of his business?

He gave the answer himself in a newspaper interview later. He said, 'To be truly human, it is necessary to care deeply for things which will not come to pass until long after we're gone.' To be truly human is to acknowledge not only a debt to the past but also some responsibility for a future one will not live to see. And had it not been for those prepared to stand for such things, we would probably still be living in caves, our minds darkened by superstition and dread.

Now, Bertrand Russell was not a believer and it would be a disservice to his memory to claim that he was one without knowing it; nevertheless, it would be hard to find a more resplendent example of that sense of responsibility for the future which characterizes religion at its best – for the Christian, the kingdom of heaven; for the Muslim, the *umma*; for the Jew, the dawn of the Messianic Age.

But what about this 'key' Levi claimed the believer possessed? Obviously there are many such keys, but the one that is common to the great religions was expressed in Jesus' words, 'Do not fear, but believe.' This is not a promise that none of the things we fear could possibly happen to us; that we are immune from unhappiness, suffering and disaster. He was not saying, 'Don't worry, it will never happen – at least not to you.' We have lived long enough to know that some of the things we most fear both can and will happen to us.

No religion that offers an escape from reality can withstand the invasion of a brutal truth. It cannot protect us from life or provide a defence against the consequences of our folly and ignorance or from natural catastrophe. Real religion will save us from fear but not from the things we are rightly afraid of. When President Franklin D. Roosevelt told the American people in the depths of the economic depression in 1933, 'The only thing we have to fear is fear itself,' he could have been paraphrasing those words of Jesus, 'Take courage; I have conquered the world' (John 16.33).

The paradoxical religious claim is that even if the worst does happen, we should not be afraid because things will come right in the end. That sounds like a crashing platitude, but in fact, it is the simple implication of belief in God, the assumption that what he started, he has the power to see through to an ordained end and can be trusted not to let things get out of control on the way. Generations of Christians have gained strength and courage from the celebrated words of Julian of Norwich, 'All shall be well, and all shall be well, and all manner of thing shall be well.' This is the conviction that life makes sense in terms of its ultimate purpose, however opaque it seems at any given moment.

'Be not afraid.' This is the rallying cry of that other war against terror, and it has no casualties, only beneficiaries.

4

The Cult of Death

In some quarters, the word 'theology' has become almost a term of abuse. When commentators regard something as rarefied, remote from the real world, purely theoretical, they say, 'Let's not get into the theology of all this. Let's stick to the point!' Well, the London suicide bombings prove that theology *is* the point; it is impossible to understand what is happening without it.

All kinds of political explanations have been offered for the motives of Al Qa'eda and its sleeper cells. Its stated goals are to drive the Americans out of Muslim societies, especially Saudi Arabia, to destroy Israel and establish a free Palestine in which the Jews would be a minority, and to restore the glory of an Islamic empire by establishing the Caliphate in states where Muslims live in significant numbers such as Pakistan, Somalia, the Philippines and Burma.

The chosen method is the act of spectacular violence, because, Al Qa'eda says, this is the only language the Americans understand and the sole weapon effective against military superpowers. It claims it is only reacting to American terrorism which has robbed the poor world of its oil and wealth, and uses force without compunction when and where it suits its interests.

It is necessary to remember that the West encouraged the creation of Al Qa'eda to suit its own strategic interests in driving the Soviet Union out of Afghanistan. US Special Forces and the Central Intelligence Agency trained the first generation of Al Qa'eda fighters in the arts of subversion and guerrilla warfare. Then, on the whirligig of the international power game, it was all-change; old enemies became friends, new enemies emerged, especially in the Middle East, but Al Qa'eda refused to remain a camp follower of the West and evolved an agenda of its own. It began to think in terms of global strategy. It saw the cold war as a clash between two materialistic godless ideologies, Communism and capitalism, both of which it despised, even though, ironically, the founder of Al Qa'eda, Osama bin Laden, is a millionaire member of an immensely wealthy family. Nevertheless, the end of the cold war appeared to create a spiritual vacuum which militant Islam could fill.

This is where theology becomes important. After Israel invaded Lebanon in 1982, Hezbollah was born and began to experiment with suicide bombings. Then the Marxist-Hindu Tamil Tigers got the message and during the 1980s killed almost 900 people, including the Indian Prime Minister, Rajiv Gandhi. But increasingly, the Islamic terrorist organizations have become the chief exponents of this lethal practice and intelligence reports suggest that from the outset there has been no shortage of volunteers. At first these volunteers tended to be single, uneducated men who might be thought to have nothing to lose, but in recent years they have been joined by the mothers of small children and highly educated professionals who apparently had much to lose. On one day in Iraq, there were 27 separate suicide bombing attacks. The suicide bomber is no longer an extremist loner; he or she is part of a growing army. One Hezbollah official has said that his problem is not to find suicide bombers but to accommodate all who are eager to join.

The influential Sunni Muslim thinker Sayyid Qutb has written: 'The Qur'an points to another contemptible characteristic of the Jews: their craven desire to live, no matter at what price and regardless of quality, honour and dignity.' Brushing aside the mandatory anti-Semitic jibe, this is a startling affirmation of the cult of death; it is a world-view in a nutshell. A common assumption in the West has been that though suicide bombers sport all the ritual and rhetoric of Islam, either their goals are strictly political or else they are fanatics, psychopaths, the most evil elements in the Arab communities. The notion that they are embracing death and bringing death to others for religious reasons is one we really don't want to believe.

Suicide bombers are not merely prepared to die in order to strike at the enemy, they want to die, to embrace death eagerly; they cannot wait to enter another world beyond the grave. An astonished police officer, having watched video footage of the four London suicide bombers at Kings Cross station just minutes before they went their separate ways to die and kill on different tube trains, said that they were laughing and joking as though they were going on holiday.

After the Al Qa'eda attack on the United States four years ago, their website said that the 9/11 bombers were now resting in paradise by cooling fountains, attended by virgins in a kingdom 'blissful and glorious'. This statement caused much hilarity in the West. Sectors of the British tabloid press had a field day, mocking Al Qa'eda not just for its savagery but also for its primitive and pornographic superstitions.

These suicide bombers believe that you enter paradise by an act of martyrdom, and you do not become a martyr by dying of old age in your bed or by jumping off Beachy Head. You become a martyr by dying in a glorious cause. Such an act short-circuits the process of divine judgement that awaits believers on the Last Day. The martyr goes directly to Allah's Garden; not for him or her to moulder in the grave until the resurrection of the dead.

This explains the fact, incomprehensible to Westerners, that the relatives of dead suicide bombers do not grieve but throw celebratory parties. This is not simply because a blow has been struck against the infidel, but because the martyr can nominate those who, when they die, will join him or her in paradise. In circles where the families of suicide bombers are treated with great respect, the actual event is known as a 'sacred explosion'.

For *Prospect* magazine (August 2005), Aatish Taseer interviewed a self-confessed British *jihadist*, Hassan Butt, who spoke openly of his intention, when the time is right, to become a suicide bomber. A graduate of Wolverhampton University, Hassan Butt, who is under investigation for links to terrorist organizations and has had his passport confiscated, gave not the slightest impression of being unbalanced or even fanatical. He is opposed to suicide attacks in Britain for tactical reasons, though he in no way condemns those who did carry out the bombings.

When Butt was asked why he intends to become a suicide bomber, he replied that there is a difference between suicide and martyrdom. Suicide is about unhappiness, depression. On the contrary, he has an urge to be in the presence of Allah, to be with the Prophet, a thought that makes him very happy. He is looking forward to death because it signifies the beginning of eternal life, and he dreads dying naturally, growing old and grey. Asked about the goal of suicide bombers, he replied, 'I don't see it happening in my lifetime. Fourteen hundred years ago, you had a small city-state in Medina and within ten years of the Prophet, Islam had spread to Egypt and all the way into Persia. I don't see why the rest of the world – the White House, 10 Downing Street – shouldn't come under the banner of Islam.'

Such a 'glorious' cause, nothing less than world domination, is obviously non-negotiable. Other terrorist organizations that employ suicide bombers, such as the Marxist-Hindu Tamil Tigers in Sri Lanka or Eta, the Basque separatist movement, have aims about which governments could argue and possibly offer some compromise, but the Islamicization of the entire West is as apocalyptic as the dreams of some Christian sects who set an early date by which they expected the kingship of glorified Christ to be universally acknowledged throughout the world. The difference is that these Christians were not prepared to employ mass murder as a mechanism by which to trigger its arrival.

It indicates how secular our society has become, so secular that many people are astonished when a young, healthy, intelligent Muslim like Hassan Butt announces that he prefers another world to the present one, or that he could even believe that this other world exists at all. Yet it is not many generations ago that devout Christians lived in the shadow of eternity, in the faith that when they died they would be with Christ in God's nearer presence. And entangled in a sinful world, they not infrequently echoed the words of the apostle Paul that they had a 'desire . . . to depart and be with Christ, for that is far better' (Philippians 1.23). Victorian Christians rhapsodized in the words of Isaac Watts about a 'Land of pure delight where saints immortal reign, where infinite day excludes the night, and pleasures banish pain'. Many Negro spirituals also expressed a yearning for a better world to which Christ's chariot would carry them up and away from their earthly misery.

Undoubtedly there is widespread anger in the world-wide Muslim community at the West's foreign policy. As Hassan Butt put it, 'With the victory [in Afghanistan] under their belt, Muslims began to realize they could control their political destiny. They woke up. You then had Iraq being attacked, you had Chechnya, Albania, Kosovo, Bosnia, Algeria, you had all these Muslim areas being attacked, and you had Muslims waking up and saying, "Hang on, this isn't a coincidence."'

A number of experts have pointed out that Islam does not distinguish between religious and civic authority, there is no equivalent in the Qur'an to those words of Jesus, 'Render to Caesar what is Caesar's and to God what is God's'; indeed, the Qur'an itself is the official constitution of Saudi Arabia. Therefore in one sense it is academic whether the suicide bomber is driven by religious or political motives. In one act, the suicide bomber strikes a blow for world domination by radical Islam and also secures his or her own eternal destiny. The lives of innocent victims are neither here nor there. They are mere props in a deadly drama.

There is a sense in which suicide bombings, however terrible their consequences, are the enactment of a fantasy. They are a grotesque form of theatre. Any political goal, the Islamicization of the whole world, is so remote that the suicide bombers couldn't seriously imagine that the deaths of 50 people on the London tube would bring it any nearer. The significance is in the act itself; it is a kind of ritual. Ritual is the ceremonial re-enactment of the stories by which we live, especially those about our origins and destiny. Ritual telescopes time, bringing the past alive and projecting the believer forward into the realm of his or her dreams.

Take a ritual at the other end of the moral spectrum from that of the suicide bomber. Christians gather round the communion table at their Lord's command not merely to re-enact the last supper of the old covenant, but also to make the imaginative leap forward to share in the first supper of the new dispensation.

Suicide bombers may feel their religion is now under threat, but by a spectacular piece of theatre they can for an instant re-enter the lost glory days when the Caliphate ruled the known world and add their lives to the toll of martyrs through whose sacrifice it will be re-established. As in classical theatre every act and word has symbolic significance. Thus, when Osama bin Laden discussed the attack on the Twin Towers in New York on video-tape, he made it clear that the original intention was not to bring about the collapse of the World Trade Centre – he assumed that it was structurally invulnerable. When the Towers did come crashing down, he was astounded and realized that it must have been due to divine intervention. The terrorists did not bring down the towers – God did. So the myth is reinforced.

Undoubtedly the widespread anger and frustration in Muslim communities at Western foreign policy may indeed be an element in the psyche of the suicide bomber, but I suspect the actual trigger is to be found in some alteration of religious consciousness, akin to conversion. Christian history testifies to the way the most unlikely people have been inspired or incited to do the most extraordinary things, for good or ill, when their lives have been changed by some kind of revelation, which can be divine or demonic. It is significant that one of the suicide bombers who attacked Madrid's transport system, killing 192 people, was a former drug dealer who had served several prison sentences. His father, who knew nothing of his son's suicidal intentions, said that his son's way of life had suddenly changed. Instead of spending time with his old underworld accomplices on the wrong side of the law, he began to attend mosque, to say prayers five times a day and to fast. He was, his father said, a changed man. Had his life ended in a genuine martyrdom, he would have been hailed as a splendid example of the converting power of religion – a notorious sinner brought to repentance.

Whatever the pious declarations of the suicide bombers, it is for Muslim scholars to judge what relationship, if any, this cult of death has to Islam and its sacred texts. I suspect that at root, this is not a case of Islam versus Christianity nor of one branch of Islam against another. At the most elemental level, it is death contending against life. Shorn of its religious mythology, suicide bombing is the embracing of chaos, the destruction of all values. Thus, the Chechnya terrorists who murdered children in the Breslan school atrocity did so, according to their spokesman, because 'Russian soldiers are killing our children in Chechnya, so we are here to kill yours.' Could there be a bleaker philosophy of life?

There is no easy cure for a love of death. It must be fought by every legal means, but the determination of the Western governments in their crusade against terrorism to restrict those civil liberties that are the strength of liberal democracy must be resisted, because our law-abiding Muslim citizens will inevitably be the chief victims, with their communities becoming the breeding ground of more suicide bombers. Governments always react to attacks on the community by more stringent anti-terror legislation, but beyond a certain point, to restrict human rights is to do Al Qa'eda's work for it.

Meanwhile, both Christians and Muslims need to revisit their doctrines of eternal life – Muslim scholars to reclaim it from the suicide bombers, while Christians need to assert and restate what is often a missing dimension in the contemporary advocacy of the gospel. At ground level, however, it is not the scholars and theologians who will decide whether the London suicide bombers were martyrs or murderers. This will be settled by the ordinary members of the Muslim communities who were shocked and puzzled by the London bombings. If significant numbers conclude the bombings were merely criminal acts, then the terrorist cells will wither and die; if it is decided otherwise, we could be in for a long period of sporadic violence.

Moderates and Extremists

In the aftermath of the London bombings, the government and the press have been appealing to 'moderate' Muslims to close ranks against the suicide bombers, who are the 'extremists' in their communities. According to this code, a moderate Muslim is one who is law-abiding, respectful of the elders of the mosque, believes that Islam is a religion of peace and is happy to co-operate with other faiths while insisting that suicide bombers are not true Muslims. Leading Muslims, defined as 'moderates', have been received at No. 10 Downing Street and consulted by government ministers about the best way to isolate and neutralize extremists.

I confess I have never heard a Muslim describe himself or herself as a 'moderate'. Try the boot on the other foot. What is a 'moderate' as opposed to an 'extreme' Christian? If we are talking about social attitudes and political opinions, many Christians would accept the label, but if 'moderate' is also meant to cover religious convictions, it suggests a conventional, rather passionless faith which takes the Bible and Christian doctrine reasonably seriously but would not go to the stake for the dot and comma of religious dogma.

And Christian extremists, who might they be? Certainly, fundamentalists, at their most rampant in the neo-con movements in the United States, but it could also include orthodox Christians who regard every clause in the creeds as God's holy truth, disdain theological liberals and believe the Church should stand out against rather than go with the flow of secular society – in other words, they boast of their commitment to full-blown Christianity.

It is therefore dangerous to pigeon-hole Muslims as either moderates or extremists and then assume these labels determine their attitudes to terrorism. Many of the Muslims regarded as moderates are utterly militant in opposition to the Iraq War and desperately exercised at the deaths of thousands of Muslims in the Middle East. On the other hand, Muslims regarded by government and police as extremists may be ranting preachers who call down fire and brimstone upon a decadent West, but it cannot be assumed that they would support suicide bombing.

There is obviously a generation dimension to this issue. Like their contemporaries in the wider community, in general, young Muslims tend to be more secular than their parents, but a significant and by all accounts growing number of them are turning to Islam because it offers them an identity and status which they believe British society has withheld from them. Unlike their parents who were first- and second-generation immigrants who had struggled to get to the United Kingdom and were proud to call themselves British, they feel themselves to be neither British nor anything else. They are too far removed from the country of their parents' birth to feel any loyalty to it.

The discovery or rediscovery of Islam, often by a process of conversion, brings discipline to lives that would otherwise seem formless, void, without boundaries. The daily prayers, fasting, observance of Ramadan and other festivals impose order on their existence, and they can feel pride in Islam's fierce traditions; they are not a disadvantaged minority but descendants of a desert warrior people. And Islam gives them a cause to serve; they identify with the struggles of Muslim societies throughout the world against their enemies, and the more alienated from the rest of British society they become, the more fervently they embrace an alternative culture which does not depend on the goodwill and tolerance of the white community.

The British intelligence services have a patchy record in the run-up to the Iraq War, but they showed prescience in warning the British government that one of the consequences of going to war against Saddam Hussein would be to radicalize young British Muslims. There is nothing 'moderate' about them, though 'devout' would be a more accurate description than 'extremist', which implies they are all potential terrorists.

This tendency of the government and the media to pigeon-hole the Muslim communities into a vast majority of moderates who believe Islam is a religion of peace, and a tiny, dangerous minority of extremists committed to *jihad*, could lead us to underestimate the dimensions of the challenge, the power and range of the *umma*, the Arabic term for the solidarity of all Muslims throughout the world and their place and purpose in the divine plan. A decade ago, Samuel Huntington reached the top of the *New York Times* Book List with a book that described the conflict between Islam and the West as a 'clash of civilizations'. He claims that dividing Muslims into moderates and extremists is to underestimate the rigour of the Islamic faith. They are all extremists in the sense that they are convinced of the superiority of their culture and the inferiority of their power. And this impotence is not felt solely by ill-educated or politically oppressed Muslims; some of those who have embraced homicidal martyrdom are professional, well-educated and affluent. So the usual nostrums proposed by the West when faced by threats to its security from restive but weaker nations – more social justice, extending democracy, forgiving debt – will not buy them off.

This is potentially an explosive state of affairs. Huntington reached his conclusions from a close study of the Qur'an. His book was attacked from all quarters, including the distinguished Arab-American Edward Said who dismissed Al Qa'eda as a bunch of 'crazed fanatics' who should be grouped with exotic groups such as the Branch Davidians and the disciples of the Reverend James Jones in Guyana who committed mass suicide.

However, the philosopher Sam Harris in *The End of Faith* thinks that Huntington is right. 'We are at war with Islam,' he writes. 'It is not merely that we are at war with an otherwise "peaceful" religion that has been hijacked by extremists. We are at war with precisely the vision of life that is prescribed to all Muslims in the Qur'an and further elaborated in the literature of the *hadith* which recounts the sayings and actions of the Prophet.'[1]

Harris criticizes what he calls 'moderate' religions such as mainstream Christianity where believers pay lip-service to their faith and are happy to have amicable discussions with their counterparts in Islam. This superficial bonhomie blinds them to the perils of fundamentalism. He says it is a mistake for Christians to imagine that Islam reflects Christianity in having a fundamentalist wing (disposed to become suicide bombers) as well as middle of the road believers who are more liberal and tolerant of other faiths. He believes almost all Muslims are fundamentalists in believing that the Qur'an is the literal and inerrant word of the one true God, and therefore it is a manifesto for militancy.

Harris concedes that there are a few lines in the Qur'an which seem to speak directly against indiscriminate violence, but he quotes pages and pages of Qur'anic verses which vilify unbelievers and consign them to the fires of hell. He says the Qur'an contains a single ambiguous line, 'Do not destroy yourselves,' which might be construed as a prohibition on suicide bombing but is outweighed by a cataract of verses in which God urges believers to mock, shame, curse, punish, scourge and annihilate infidels.

Certainly obedience to every letter of the Qur'an has produced some dramatic and bizarre news items which reinforce this impression of social oppression. There was violence in Nigeria in 2002 when the 'Miss World' competition was being held in

---

1 Sam Harris, *The End of Faith*, The Free Press, 2005, p. 235.

the capital, Abuja. A local newspaper criticized Muslim groups who were protesting against the contestants parading half-naked. It opined, 'What would the prophet Muhammad think? In all honesty, he would probably have chosen a wife from among the contestants.' This outraged the Muslim population and in the resulting riots over 200 people were killed or injured as young men shouting '*Allahu Akhbar*' or 'God is great!' rampaged through the streets beating to death innocent bystanders and burning down Christian churches.

That same year, the religious police in Mecca prevented fire-fighters and paramedics from rescuing a number of teenage girls trapped in a burning dormitory because, having been asleep, they would not be wearing the head covering that the Qur'an requires.

Of course, these are extreme examples of religious pathology which are not unique to Islam. Most of the suicide bombers in the Lebanese war in the early 1980s came from the Christian community; Hindus committed large-scale atrocities against Muslims during the partition of India. There is a dark side to all religions – certainty hardens into fanaticism and zeal becomes aggression.

Some of the most serious misunderstandings about the present crisis arise because commentators fail to recognize that there is good and bad religion, just as there is good and bad science, art and politics. Religion is treated as something that simply exists and people must either be for it or against it. So no distinction is made between religious activities that are right and those that are wrong, between religious assertions that are true and those that are false, between religious emotions that are healthy and those that are vicious. It is impossible to justify religion as a whole; it is only what is valid that can or ought to be defended. In his book *Violence in God's Name*, Oliver McTernan writes:

> The political and social milieu may act as a trigger for people
> compelled to kill in the name of their God, but the roots of

religious intolerance and militancy are embedded in the history and sacred texts of the world's faiths. Today's extremists can find in their own traditions sufficient texts and in their own religious history sufficient exemplars to justify their adoption of a world view that allows them to annihilate those who think or act differently.[2]

As an outsider, I am not qualified to judge how true is Sam Harris' claim that 'On almost every page, the Qur'an instructs observant Muslims to despise non-believers. On almost every page, it prepares the ground for religious conflict.' One respected Arab commentator, Abdul Rahman al-Rashid, has said, 'It is a certain fact that not all Muslims are terrorists, but it is equally certain, and exceptionally painful, that almost all terrorists are Muslims.'

That is not strictly true. The Tamil Tigers in Sri Lanka are Hindu Marxists; Eta, the Basque Separatist Movement in Spain, is secular, but it is true that the grievances and operating areas of these movements are strictly local, and unless outsiders are unlucky enough to be caught in the wrong place at the wrong time they would be unaffected. Only Muslim terrorists claim to be engaged in a global war.

But Christians ought to feel no sense of moral superiority about the harsh attacks on infidels prescribed in the Qur'an. There are passages in the Bible where unbelievers are threatened with the direst consequences. In the Old Testament God wipes out communities with fire and pestilence. Jesus' namesake, the great hero Joshua, massacred the whole population of Jericho because of their 'impiety' with the evident approval of Yahweh (Joshua 6). Commenting on some Psalms, C. S. Lewis wrote, 'The spirit of hatred which strikes us in the face is like heat from a furnace mouth.' The apostle Paul, too, in his Letter to the Romans is merciless in his

---

2 Oliver McTernan, *Violence in God's Name*, Darton, Longman & Todd, 2003, p. 144.

condemnation of unbelievers. 'Because they have not seen fit to acknowledge God, he has given them up to their depraved reason. They are filled with every kind of injustice, mischief, rapacity and malice. They are one mass of envy, murder, treachery and malevolence' (Romans 1.28–9).[3] And in that denouement of history foretold in the Book of Revelation, unbelievers are consigned with murderers, fornicators, sorcerers and liars to the lake burning with fire and brimstone, the second death (Revelation 21.8). Little wonder that a Christian so orthodox as John Wesley could rule that some passages in the Bible are not fit to be read in public worship.

There have periods in the Church's history when the threat of hell-fire was the key-signature of evangelism, but most modern Christians either skip quickly over these blood-thirsty passages or else subject them to reinterpretation, judging the lowest expressions of the divine will by the highest, the harshest portrayals of God giving way to the most loving, compassionate and forgiving.

Professor Mona Siddiqui says that Islam has an intellectual tradition where the scholars have had for centuries a monopoly over learning; it is precisely because people didn't interpret the Qur'an as they wished that an integrity of thought and commentary stayed in the hands of the few, not preventing the masses from piety and freedom of worship but preventing rogue dimensions to divine scripture.

But the pressures both of modern culture and of world events are forcing Muslim scholars and imams to seek new interpretations of the Qur'an. Thus, in the aftermath of the London bombings, one of the most senior Muslim scholars in Britain, Dr Zaki Badawi, pronounced that because Muslim women were being subjected to harassment in public places, they need not wear the *hijab* or headscarf which identifies them, even though the Qur'an

---

3 Translation from Graham Shaw, *The Cost of Authority*, SCM Press, 1983.

specifically demands it. He explained that the purpose of the *hi-jab* is to protect Muslim women and therefore his advice is in line with the Qur'an's intention, even though it is at odds with the actual text. Most Muslim women, however, rejected Dr Badawi's proposal, insisting that, whatever the social consequences, they would prefer to obey holy writ rather than reinterpret it. This is merely a single instance of a debate which is ranging ever wider within Islam. And the agonizing will be particularly intense about those texts which might be used to justify violence against infidels.

Because we are anxious to maintain good community relations and extend ecumenical co-operation with other faiths, these conclusions are not palatable to us. We choose to believe that 'moderate' Muslims, who abhor violence and are radiant examples of a kinder, more tolerant Islam represent the norm whereas the militants are driven by political ambitions and anti-West hatred. But sooner or later we shall have to face head-on the challenge that Harris and McTernan state in such stark terms. Harris writes:

> Religious violence is with us and will grow because religions are *intrinsically* hostile to one another. When they appear otherwise, it is because secular knowledge and secular interests are restraining the most lethal improprieties of faith. It is time we acknowledged that no real foundation exists within the canons of Christianity, Islam, Judaism, or any other faiths, for religious tolerance and religious diversity.[4]

This is no esoteric theological issue. The recent attack on London brings home to us that the challenge is not to repel murderous invaders, to keep out and neutralize insurgents. Besides the wisdom and morality of our foreign policy, our peace and security could depend upon the outcome of our neighbours' study of the sacred texts of Islam.

---

4 Harris, *The End of Faith*, p. 225.

The Dead, Too, Have Their Rights

Though television cameras were on the scene of the London bombings in a remarkably short time, the public was protected from the more horrific images of broken and mutilated bodies because of the speed and sensitivity with which the Metropolitan Police erected canvas screens round the wreckage of the No. 30 bus and at the entrances to the tube stations where bombs had gone off. Thus, the bodies of the dead could be recovered and removed in privacy. This may seem a minor decency amid the chaos, but it represents an important principle – that the dead have rights, one of which is to have their dignity protected for them when they are in no position to do it for themselves.

This is not a courtesy universally observed. The visible body count of the Iraq War has been horrendous – Saddam's victims, layer upon layer, rotting in mass graves; the casualties of car bombings, charred and barely human, dragged out of the grotesquely distorted skeletons of what were once their vehicles; civilians buried under the wreckage of the homes, reduced to rubble by missiles fired by the coalition forces or smashed down by their tanks. Then there are the neat rows of body bags, each carefully tagged and wrapped in the Stars and Stripes on the runway of US air force bases, dead American soldiers awaiting repatriation home.

In the early days of cinema newsreels and then television news bulletins there were very strict rules prohibiting close-up pictures of dead bodies. There were still taboos operating in society, forbidden areas it was not decent for the public to trespass upon. Taboos mark out boundaries we agree not to cross because experience teaches that beyond them lies moral disintegration.

As the news footage of the London bombings demonstrates, we still preserve some reticence about showing explicit images of the newly dead on home television here in Britain; screens are erected, bodies are rapidly covered up, the camera glances away quickly. But there is no such punctiliousness about news footage shot in faraway places. Bulletin by bulletin, several times a day we see the dead lying hideously exposed, unnoticed in life, but in death observed by millions.

This is death as a public spectacle. And the most dramatic of these images of the moment of death have become iconic, being replayed over and over again – President John F. Kennedy in Dallas putting his hand up to his head and his wife staring incredulously at her blood-splattered dress; the US space shuttle 'Challenger' disintegrating in mid-air shortly after take-off, so that its crew died the most public deaths in the history of the world as hundreds of millions of TV viewers watched. Then there was the moment when Donald Campbell's speed-boat 'Bluebird' launched itself like a guided missile from the surface of Lake Windermere; and that scratchy film of the airship 'Hindenburg' about to tie up in New York, suddenly becoming a glowing, skeletal lantern and crumpling like charred paper to the ground. These events only happened once but they have been endlessly replayed.

The war on terrorism too has produced its iconic death images, which we have seen repeatedly. As the Twin Towers were about to collapse in a bedlam of smoke and flame, there were those tiny figures shown jumping out of windows a thousand feet from the ground, some holding hands, having made the nightmare decision to die on the concrete rather than be burned alive by blazing aircraft fuel. Then after the Iraq War began, there were the bodies of Saddam's two sons, lying side by side in a makeshift mortuary, proudly displayed by the Americans; the more spectacular car-bombing victims; and the shot of an American soldier, burnt black, being hauled out of the turret of a tank that had been hit by a missile; the Kurds gassed by Saddam lying in the streets like discarded heaps of clothes. And the mass graves opened and excavated.

Again and again we are shown these pictures because they prove a point; they illustrate why we are in Iraq, the evil that was Saddam and paradoxically, the justification for our side adding to the number of bodies littering the landscape. This is not just death as public spectacle but also as propaganda.

We may first see these very public deaths as news, but they end up as newszak. Newszak is to news what Muzak is to music. Muzak is all that is left of music when its performance ceases to be an occasion and becomes a background, an interminable flood of sound, fitfully recognizable, that floats in and out of our consciousness. Muzak is the husk of music, what is left after its emotional power has been discharged. It is used to fill the air waves of a society that cannot stand silence.

As a parallel, newszak is the husk of news – events drained of topicality, moments evacuated of their original horror, splendour or interest; sensations that have lost the sting of immediate impact but are still used to make a point or sway public opinion.

But when the content of newszak is someone's real-life death, then we are flouting an ultimate taboo. The forbidden sights modern society prefers to hide away behind hospital bed screens now implode into viewers' sitting rooms. Our forebears confronted death as a common public occurrence. So does our society, but it lacks the theological framework, that mélange of liturgy, hymnody, faith, superstition and folk wisdom that enabled previous generations to make sense of it.

It is neither possible nor desirable for news bulletins to become electronic versions of the original *Christian Science Monitor*, a newspaper, it is alleged, that firmly excluded death, disaster, war and unhappiness from its columns. In which case, there needs to be a much clearer recognition of these rights of the dead – to dignity, to privacy, to freedom from the endless re-enactment for ulterior purposes of the moment of their passing.

The old rubrics referred to the 'sacred' dead, to signify that here was a mystery in whose presence one should tread with care. Since they cannot preserve their own dignity nor hide their awful helplessness, it is the duty of the living to protect them. The same impulse of charity that would have us clothe the naked and bind up the wounds of the broken also impels us to show mercy to those being humiliated through exposure to the public gaze.

There are some taboos rooted in superstition and prudery that should be swept away; there are areas of unnecessary secrecy that need to have daylight let in on them. But other taboos came into being to guard sacred mysteries, and that surrounding what the liturgy calls the 'holy' dead is one. Our lives have mysterious depths because a little bit of God's infinite dignity is woven into human nature. The callous flaunting of images of the dead is literally shameful.

The Language of War

A row has broken out between the BBC and one of our tabloid newspapers which claimed that the broadcasters in using the term 'bombers' to describe those who attacked London were being mealy-mouthed. They were 'terrorists', snarled the *Sun*, and that's all there is to it. But then the IRA announced that after 30 years it had finally abandoned the armed struggle for a united Ireland. In welcoming the statement, the appropriate minister referred to the IRA as a 'para-military organization', though some years ago when Canary Wharf was blown up, the government talked about an 'act of terrorism'.

Shortly after the Iraq War started, an Iraqi soldier, a suicide bomber, killed himself and four marines. The Americans called it an act of terrorism. The Iraqis, on the other hand, spoke of his heroism and awarded him a posthumous decoration. A coalition spokesman then said that only criminal elements of the Iraqis who have nothing to lose were still resisting, but correspondents on the front line say that significant numbers of Iraqis seem to be fighting and dying in defence of their homeland. So, what was the truth of it – terrorists or heroes? Party lackeys or patriots?

The international war against terror is being fought not only across the world but also within the pages of the dictionary. If, as the cliché has it, truth is the first casualty of war, then language is the second – words used by both sides, which hide rather than reveal the reality of what is going on.

Take the bureaucratic jargon used during the Iraq conflict to soften the sharp edge off the killing trade. Weapons became 'systems', tanks and planes were 'assets', civilians killed or injured constituted 'collateral damage'. Soldiers did not kill their enemy, they 'degraded his war-making capacity'. The coalition forces were trying to avoid 'breaking the china', that is, laying waste to cities and towns. The Americans would have broken a lot of china if they had used the biggest of their explosive devices which they christened 'the Mother of all Bombs'. Saddam Hussein too was apparently fond of the same image: he boasted of the coming 'Mother of all Battles'. It seems obscene to link motherhood, whose essence is to nurture life, with either a super bomb or an operation aimed at destroying life.

Then there is the tragically ironic phrase, 'friendly fire' – which implies it is more bearable to be killed or wounded through the mistakes or accidents of our own side than by the malice of our enemies. When that happens, it is known in military code as a 'blue on blue'. And I heard a new one when an RAF officer described how a NATO guided missile was deflected. It was, he said, 'seduced from its target'. Even the language of courtship and love is conscripted to the cause.

The greatest controversy attaches to the terms 'terrorism' and 'terrorists'. After the 9/11 atrocity, the official party line in the United States was initially that those who attacked the Twin Towers were psychopaths, 'mindless sadists' as one Congressman described them. Then the evidence revealed that they were in fact highly educated, intelligent men who calmly went about their task with almost boring efficiency; they took over passenger jets and turned them into missiles.

And the weapons they used to penetrate the defences of the mightiest military complex in the world were no more lethal than knives and airline tickets. Their brain power and ingenuity were striking. The accepted stereotype of the terrorist as a poor, naïve and desperate Third World fanatic brainwashed to hate the West was shattered as intelligence reports revealed that the typical recruit to Al Qa'eda was likely to be from the upper middle classes, probably a professional and drawn from one of the wealthier Arab countries.

By definition, a terrorist is someone who engages in revolutionary violence aimed at destroying the morale of an enemy nation by the random murder of innocent people. And an additional lethal dimension has been added to modern terrorism by the suicide bomber who lays down his or her life in order to kill others. Some romantics would say that the suicide bomb is the only effective weapon the weak can use against the strong. It is a desperate balancing of power – overwhelming military force versus ultimate sacrifice.

Following President Bush's declaration of war on international terrorism, the term 'terrorism' took on an expanded meaning, to include not just the men who attacked the Twin Towers but any group, anywhere in the world, fighting against their government – for example, Basque Separatists in Spain, Tamil Tigers in Sri Lanka and Chechnyan rebels in Russia. All the nations who signed up to President Bush's crusade were able to incorporate their internal conflicts into a general struggle, even though the causes and cures might be different in each case. Issues of great complexity were reduced to a simple equation: struggles against established authority were by definition assaults by evil upon good.

With the rise of Al Qa'eda, terrorism has taken on a new and apocalyptic dimension. Al Qa'eda calls its driving ideology radical Islam which is destined to replace the spiritual emptiness of the West, though many Muslim scholars deny that what Al Qa'eda is doing can be reconciled with their understanding of the holy books of Islam.

The tragedy is that in a conflict where not only human beings but language have suffered, 'terrorism' and 'Islam' have become fused, the one word trips off the tongue automatically after the other – a conjunction that is unjust and untrue, but the damage has been done.

It is a minor part of the struggle against terrorism but an important one to use words fastidiously, on the one hand to avoid the slick euphemisms that hide the awful realities of war, and on the other, to keep apart terms that do not necessarily belong together. Bishop John Austin Baker says this about the relationship between truth and the words in which it is stated: 'Thoughts are not expressed in words – they exist in words and only in words. Truth does not come to men clothed in words. It comes to them as words; and when as far as possible we know what the words mean, then as far as possible we know what the truth is to them.'[1]

Words don't just describe the truth; they embody it, which is why we must use them with care. The New Testament scholar Amos Wilder claims that in primitive societies, people do not first see an object and then give it a name. In naming it they call it into being. 'If the naming of things is equivalent to their being called into being, we find ourselves on the same ground with the Genesis account of creation. God spoke and it was done. Such is the power of the word. Islam has a tradition that if one could stumble on the right word and speak it, the whole universe would vanish in a moment. The word is sovereign.'[2]

Christians have a particular responsibility because some of their forebears spilt blood in defence of religious concepts which some puzzled observers would have called mere words. Sam Harris is harsh in his judgement of liberal or what he calls 'moderate' Christians who are not fastidious about words; who for the best of motives deliberately use language loosely in order to bridge gaps and reconcile extremes. Imprecise language implies vague religious truths which are not sharply enough defined to challenge the harsh and dogmatic convictions of the

1 John Austin Baker, *The Foolishness of God*, Darton, Longman & Todd, 1971, p. 364.

2 Amos Wilder, *Early Christian Rhetoric*, SCM Press, 1964, p. 14.

extremists. 'Religious moderates are, in large part, responsible for the religious conflict in our world, because their beliefs provide the context in which scriptural literalism and religious violence can never be adequately opposed.'[3]

We are, to use a hackneyed phrase in a more deadly sense, truly engaged in a war of words.

---

3 Harris, *The End of Faith*, p. 20.

On Criticizing Israel

In July 2005 relations between the state of Israel and the Vatican reached a low ebb following a statement by Pope Benedict about suicide attacks. A bitter exchange of views erupted when the Pope deplored terrorist attacks in Egypt, Turkey, Iraq and Britain, but made no mention of a suicide bombing that same week which killed five Israelis at Netanya.

The Israeli Foreign Minister demanded an explanation, adding that 'not condemning terrorism has been the Vatican's policy for years. Now we have a new Pope we have decided to confront this question.' The Vatican issued a strongly worded defence of Pope Benedict's original statement, saying that he omitted any mention of Israel and Palestine in the condemnation because Israel 'sometimes retaliated to attacks in ways not always compatible with the rules of international law. It would thus be impossible to condemn the Palestinian attacks and let the Israeli retaliation pass in silence.'

Most governments would probably have maintained a dignified silence in the face of criticism such as that of the Vatican, dismissing it as part of the knock-about of international relations, but the Israeli government is relentless not just in countering any criticism of its policies but also in ascribing them to anti-Semitism. And since it is generally agreed that the root of the ferment in the Middle East is the Israeli–Palestinian conflict, Israel will be constantly in the spotlight. The arguments are well trodden. Most Arab states dispute Israel's right to exist and are prepared to back terrorist movements seeking its extinction. As recently as October 2005, the President of Iran called for Israel to be 'wiped off the face of the map'. His remarks were greeted with widespread enthusiasm in his own country, while most nations condemned him.

On the other hand much of the world is appalled at Israel's treatment of the Palestinians, the military occupation of their territory, the daily humiliation they endure at check-points, the assassination missile strikes against their leaders. The Israelis retort by pointing to the almost daily suicide attacks on Jewish civilians, the refusal of the Palestinians to observe peace treaties, not to mention their own internal problems with a powerful lobby of right-wing Zionists who oppose any peace settlement that might force them to give up territory taken over from the Palestinians.

The philosopher John Gray has written that in the end, all modern conflicts are wars of scarcity, particularly to do with oil and water. At the heart of the Israeli–Palestinian conflict is a struggle over land and water. There are two powerful competing claims for a small piece of territory, which to the Jews is their biblical homeland, and to the Palestinians ground they have farmed for centuries and from which they are now excluded except under rigorously controlled conditions. What elevates the conflict into a religious tragedy is that this tiny patch of earth houses some of the holiest sites for Judaism, Christianity and Islam. And the stakes have been raised by America's massive economic, military and diplomatic support for Israel, vetoing critical resolutions at the UN and issuing regular threats against her Arab neighbours. It is a firmly held conviction among many Arabs that the American-led invasion of Iraq had the twofold purpose of securing oil supplies and neutralizing a military power that might prove a threat to Israel.

According to the Torah, there is an inextricable link between land and people, but the very actions the Israelis are using to hold on to the land are condemned in holy writ. Even over land, human life is sovereign. The Palestinian radical group Hamas also claims the land of Palestine as an Islamic *Waaf,* or holy possession. Religion is at the root of the land question.

I am only now concerned with a minor detail of this intractable conflict, the one highlighted by the row between the Vatican and the Israeli government. When the occasion arises, how is it possible to be critical of any of the policies of Israel's government without being accused of anti-Semitism and giving aid and comfort to those who wish to see Israel obliterated? Israel itself is quick to accuse its detractors of anti-Semitism, so does this mean that the normal processes of responsible critical debate must be suspended because of the fear that false conclusions will be drawn from what is said in good faith and with no ulterior motive?

There is an immensely powerful Jewish lobby in Britain and America determined to protect and counter any criticism of Israel. This is understandable, because in the 1930s when the Jews in Europe stood alone and were picked off nation by nation, there was no international lobby to intercede on their behalf. Few people spoke up for them, the world went on its way uninterested. Their descendants are determined that this will not happen again. So, criticize Israel and you run the gauntlet of this intellectual and political defence force.

Without doubt, there is a rising tide of anti-Semitism in the West. The Community Security Trust, which is a body that monitors anti-Semitism, reports that abusive and violent attacks on British Jews reached record levels in 2004. Some of these attacks were fuelled by the Middle East conflict, as opponents of Israel took their anger out on British Jews. In its nastiest form, anti-Semitism surfaced during the 2005 General Election when a pressure group, MPAC, targeted Jewish MPs with the aim of 'eliminating all pro-Israel, Zionist MPs from power'. One MP was described as a 'Zionist Islamophobe', another, 'a Zionist scumbag' and his seat was described as 'Tel Aviv South'. Missiles were thrown at Oona King, the half-black, half-Jewish MP for Bethnal Green. And there is a perpetual rash of desecration of Jewish graves.

Far from being anti-Semitic, I owe to the Jews more than I can say – my moral values, my philosophy of life, even the sense of justice I try to bring to bear on the Israeli-Palestinian conflict. All these were given to me by Jews: Jesus of Nazareth, Paul of Tarsus, the Old Testament prophets. They shaped my faith and educated my conscience. But it's not just to great historical Jewish figures that I am indebted. There was the community rabbi in Manchester who taught me Hebrew and much else besides; Jewish friends who showed me what generosity of spirit and sheer humanity look like. And I've learned much from those Jewish theologians who wrestled with that appalling question: 'Where was God in the death camps?' Out of their agonizing have come some of the most profound and important theological ideas of our time. Our spirits have been enriched by the reflections of those who suffered agonies beyond belief.

As the American lawyer Alan Dershowitz has pointed out in defence of Israel, 'No other nation in history faced with comparable challenges has ever adhered to a higher standard of human rights, been more sensitive to the safety of innocent civilians, tried harder to operate under the rule of law, or been willing to take more risks for peace.'[1] The strength of that democracy to withstand immense strains is bound to be tested to the limit as Jewish settlers are removed from the Gaza Strip in accordance with the road map to peace. Many of them are religious zealots who firmly believe that God will intervene to frustrate the efforts of the Israeli army and police.

My debt to the Jews is inexhaustible. But for a handful of Jews there would have been no Christianity. This is a fascinating historical conjecture. Had all Jews accepted Jesus as Messiah there would be no Christianity; the life, death and teaching of Jesus

---

1 Quoted by Harris, *The End of Faith*, p. 192.

would have been incorporated into Judaism. If, on the other hand, no Jews had accepted Jesus as Messiah, again, there would have been no Christianity, for (with one or two exceptions) the earliest Christians were Jews.

It was the Jewish prophets who taught me that no nation, not even that of God's elect, can be beyond moral judgement. They were much harder on their own people than they were on the so-called heathen nations. Amos reports this word from God, 'You only have I known of all the families of the earth; therefore I will punish you for all your iniquities' (Amos 3.2). Granted, the prophets were Jews speaking to other Jews, and you could say that only those who share a common heritage and fate with Israel have the right to criticize her. For instance, the Jewish scholar and writer Elie Wiesel says, 'If I want to criticize Israel, I go to Israel.' Any such visit would be a prophetic act on his part; for the rest of us, it would be sheer exhibitionism, inviting a show-piece martyrdom for the benefit of the media. However, if Jews and non-Jews can only make moral judgements about their own kind, how will we ever develop a sense of international responsibility?

There are fundamentalist Christians who support Israel for utterly cynical motives. They oppose the modest land for peace policy which would involve Israel withdrawing from territory they occupied after the Six Day War. They want Israel to wipe out the enemies that threaten the sovereignty of the Holy Land and the Holy City. This, they believe, will trigger the Second Coming of Christ, one consequence of which will be to spell the end of Jewry, whose very existence is a living affront to the Messiahship of Christ. They believe support for Israel is a biblically sanctioned foreign policy until such time as the glorious return of Christ renders the Jewish people expendable.

The loathsome spectre of anti-Semitism never goes away, so any criticism of Israel must be sensitive to the fact that the destiny of Jews everywhere and the destiny of that one state are inextricably linked. I doubt any non-Jew can really understand the scar that the Holocaust left on the Jewish psyche. At Auschwitz alone, over a million children died, not because of their faith nor in spite of their faith. They paid the price for the faith of their great-grand-parents, who refused to abandon their Jewishness and assimilate with the European peoples among whom they lived. After the Holocaust, it is an extraordinary act of faith for parents to bring up their children as Jews. For what guarantee can there be that somewhere, at some future time, the unspeakable may not occur – that any Jew may be condemning his or her great-grandchildren to a re-enactment of the same horror? Which is why Jews believe the state of Israel must be defended as the final refuge the victims of the Holocaust never had.

Far from seeking to undermine the state of Israel, many Christians hope that Israel will begin to show by her actions that in the words of that ancient hymn the Nunc Dimittis, she is a light to lighten the Gentiles.

Seven Devils

Arguments rage not only in political circles but in the community at large about the relationship of cause and effect, if any, between the London bombings and the war in Iraq. Opponents of the war claim that the coalition forces' attack on Iraq followed by the deaths of tens of thousands of civilians has angered Muslims throughout the world and acted as a recruiting agency for Al Qa'eda. The critics say that Britain's support for the United States has made this country a prime target for terrorist attack. The government rejects this contention, insisting that Al Qa'eda was bombing targets throughout the world before the Iraq War began. In any case, they argue, even if the war against Iraq made it more likely that London would be the target for terrorists, that does not necessarily mean that the war was in itself wrong.

What makes the issue even more contentious is that the legality of the war is still hotly contested. The professors of law are at odds, and leaked documents suggest that the Attorney General, whose grave duty it was to pronounce on the legality of the war, either changed his mind or at least had serious reservations about the attack on Saddam Hussein's regime.

This is not simply a matter of law; it goes to the heart of the theology of the state. Saddam Hussein had been in breach of UN resolutions and subjected some of his people to the most brutal repression, but as some legal experts pointed out, without specific UN authorization (the so-called second resolution which the US and Britain were unable to obtain) the West had declared war on a sovereign state and one much weaker than itself. According to the British Prime Minister, the invasion was justified because the Iraqis had weapons of mass destruction and were capable of launching them against Britain in 45 minutes. First, UN inspectors and then the Americans and British finally conceded that at the time of the invasion of Iraq, no such weapons existed, though they believe Saddam did possess them but had destroyed them.

Saddam Hussein obtained power by a military coup, maintained it by repressive force and denied his people any democratic rights. But the same could be said of half a dozen unpleasant dictators whom the West still calls allies. The plain fact is that Saddam's regime was recognized by the UN as the lawful authority in Iraq.

Here is the theological issue. Where does the state, any state including that of Saddam Hussein, get its authority from? Greek philosophers such as Aristotle said that the human desire for order and protection requires a rational pattern to be imposed on communal life, and this is what the state does. Reformation theologians like Martin Luther saw the origins of the state in the Fall, when the pattern of divine order was broken up and chaos reigned. The state was needed to keep corrupt human nature in check. Martin Luther wrote: 'If there were no worldly government, no man could live because of other men; one would devour the other as brute beasts do, so it is the function and honour of earthly government to make men out of wild beasts and to prevent men from becoming wild beasts.'

On this view, the state is a sword-bearer to safeguard life and punish sin. The New Testament, however, offers a more positive estimate – the authority of the state comes from God: as Jesus said to Pilate, 'You would have no power over me unless it had been given you from above' (John 19.11). The apostle Paul puts the matter squarely: 'Let every person be subject to the governing authorities; for there is no authority except from God, and those authorities that exist have been instituted by God. Therefore whoever resists authority resists what God has appointed, and those who resist will incur judgement' (Romans 13.1–2). It couldn't be spelled out more bluntly than that.

For Paul and those to whom he was writing, this issue wasn't just a matter of idle speculation. What was to be the attitude of the early Church to the Roman Empire under whose rule it lived? Jewish national feeling was running high and brewed up into a crisis in 66 CE. Many Jewish Christians resented the Romans; indeed, a stream of virulent hatred against Rome runs through the Revelation of St John, though that book was written during a period when active persecution of Christians had become imperial policy. But even when Christianity had been outlawed, Paul still insisted that a duty of loyalty was owed to the state, though Christians must reject Caesar-worship.

Paul points out that it is the *existing* authorities which are ordained of God, not some ideal state of our hopes and dreams. It is any state, anywhere, at any time, which must be accorded honour and obedience. In the very act of existing, whether it is good, bad or indifferent, the state fulfils a divine function. This doesn't mean that we cannot make ethical judgements about it. Christians may find themselves, in loyalty to the gospel, disobeying particular laws of a government, but this does not absolve them from loyalty in other aspects of its life. Ponder these words of Dietrich Bonhoeffer who paid with his life for an act of defiance against Hitler: 'No matter if a man's path to government office repeatedly passes through guilt, no matter if every crown is stained with guilt, the being of government lies beyond its earthly coming into being . . . An ethical failure does not in itself deprive a government of its divine dignity.'[1]

What applied to Paul's Rome, equally applies to Saddam Hussein's Iraq. It is at this moment a lawful government, guilty of

---

1 Dietrich Bonhoeffer, *Ethics*, SCM Press, 1955, p. 304.

the most appalling crimes for which Saddam must be punished, and the international community is slowly evolving ways of bringing those who commit mass crimes to account. But his acts were *crimes*, and to turn the whole thing into a full-blown war in which it is certain that many innocent people will die, fuels the suspicion of sceptics that there is in play another agenda to do with oil supplies and creating a *cordon sanitaire* around America's great ally, Israel.

As a matter of historical fact, Saddam's worst crimes were committed years before the invasion. The mass killing of the Kurds took place in 1988; in 1991 he put down a rising of his Shia people with great brutality and persecuted marsh Arabs in the mid-1990s. A good case for military intervention could have been made at any of those times. Since the end of the worst times in Iraq, there have been genocides in Rwanda and widespread repression in Burma, North Korea and Turkmenistan with no suggestion of American military action.

In other words, the case for invading Iraq was much weaker when the war actually began than it had been some years earlier. This is not to defend Saddam Hussein but simply to argue that the West's reasons for invading a sovereign state are nothing like as morally transparent as President Bush has made out. And to add irony to tragedy, Osama bin Laden, against whose movement President Bush has declared a global war, is Saddam Hussein's bitterest enemy, and Iraq is one of the few Middle East states where Al Qa'eda had been unable to get a foothold. Despite exhaustive enquiries by US intelligence, not a shred of evidence has been found linking Saddam Hussein to the 9/11 attacks on New York and Washington. In the Alice in Wonderland logic of this whole mess, Saddam had been fighting Al Qa'eda for longer than President Bush and is then attacked as bin Laden's accomplice and soul mate.

Iraq, besides being a sovereign state, is also a secular one, a rare situation in the Middle East. Unlike the situation in next-door

Iran, the mullahs of militant Islam have been unable to impose a puritanical social order based on their understanding of *sharia* law on Iraq. As a secularist, Saddam had been widely despised in the Muslim world prior to the invasion, but the idea of an army of Western infidels occupying Baghdad won him enough sympathy to outweigh the fact that he had a unique record in murdering Muslims.

Which takes us back to Paul. He defended the institution of the state because he had the political realism to see that though citizens might suffer badly in an authoritarian state, they would suffer worse if there were no state at all. Tyranny may be awful but anarchy is much worse – a condition classically described in the Old Testament: 'In those days there was no king in Israel; all the people did what was right in their own eyes' (Judges 21.25).

I saw anarchy at close quarters in the Congo in 1960–61. There was no law and order, no police, soldiers were fighting among themselves, criminals pouring out of gaols, the strong freed from all restraints preying like wild beasts on the weak; the people were like frightened sheep, without leaders, scattering in all directions. In Rwanda, 30 years later, when the nation dissolved into chaos, almost a million people were butchered while a small UN force stood by helpless.

Things may be hard for some under a repressive regime, yet a life of sorts is possible, but when anarchy reigns, it is back to the jungle for all, at the mercy of the big beasts. In the Christian tradition from Paul onwards and through Augustine, tyranny has always been accounted a lesser sin than anarchy. As William Tyndale declared in his *Obedience of a Christian Man*: 'It is better to have a tyrant for a king than a shadow, for a tyrant, though he do wrong to the good, yet he punisheth the evil and maketh men obey. A king who is soft as silk shall be more grievous to the realm than a right tyrant.'

The first duty of the state is to survive with enough power to hold together all the competing groups with private interests, and to enforce uniform submission to the law, however repressive that law might be. The social virtues such as justice, democracy and freedom may be curtailed in an authoritarian state, but they will vanish altogether if the state collapses.

Therefore the coalition forces must recognize the consequences when Saddam Hussein's government was overthrown. He had held together with ruthless force a nation that was artificially created by imperial Britain. The Kurds in the north, the Sunnis of the central area and the Shia in the south have a long history of mutual antipathy. The Shia and Sunni compete for dominance as the official wing of Islam while the Kurds have no desire to be part of Iraq at all. The notion that when the strong arm of Saddam was removed and his state collapsed, ordinary Iraqis would come together peacefully and joyfully to set up some version of Western democracy was highly optimistic, even before the coalition forces inflicted heavy casualties on the population in order to dislodge Saddam's forces.

There was something demonic about the way Saddam Hussein treated his people and the neighbours in Iran with whom he went to war, but Jesus once told a story about such a demon. He described a room occupied by a single devil which the householder swept clean, whereupon seven other devils rushed in to fill the vacuum, and the 'the last state of that person is worse than the first' (Matthew 12.45). Critics of the war would say that this is precisely the situation in Iraq at the present time. Not only was the regime of Saddam Hussein removed but the whole framework of civic order was demolished. The police and armed forces were disbanded, 400,000 of them, without pay or pensions, but because America supports private gun ownership, they were allowed to keep their weapons. Criminals were released from gaol, civil servants who kept the machine of government running were dismissed, the officials who ran the public services responsible for supplying water and electricity were got rid of – because all of them had been members of Saddam's Ba'athist party.

The result has been that whole areas of Iraq are in a state of near chaos. As a US senator put it, 'We are dealing with a population that hovers between bare intolerance and outright hostility. The idea of a functioning democracy is crazy. All hell is breaking loose.' The coalition forces are likely to be mired there for the foreseeable future in spite of the formal declaration of the end of the war. As the Pentagon itself has admitted, it is now fighting not a disaffected rabble but a 'thinking and adaptive' enemy. In spite of well-attended elections, the unitary state is in danger of fragmenting as Sunni, Shia and Kurd are unable to agree on important articles in a new draft constitution to do with women's rights, regional power and whether Iraq should be renamed as an Islamic republic.

Iraq has attracted insurgents from many parts of the world, eager to die in order to kill infidels. Every month in Iraq, there are more suicide bombings than Israel has suffered in a decade. General Muhammad Abdullah Shahwani, the chief of Iraqi intelligence, reckons there are 200,000 active fighters in the insurgency. The country has become a sort of military academy where the lessons learned on the battlefield can be taken back home by these guerrilla fighters.

Seven devils have been let loose with a vengeance; and perhaps the seventh is to be found in the growing number of our home-grown citizens who see themselves not as British but as defenders of a global Muslim community threatened by the oppression of the West. And tragically, the anger of some has turned homicidal.

Much of the new anti-terror legislation proposed by the Prime Minister assumes that Al Qa'eda masterminds are fomenting violence among home-grown Muslims and then directing their bombing operations: destroy or neutralize these evil men and you break the back of the problem. The much more fearsome possibility is that the four London bombers were self-motivated. The youngest, who blew himself up on the No. 30 bus in Tavistock

Square, was just 18, much too young to have been indoctrinated by Al Qa'eda in Afghanistan; another, Germaine Lindsay, was the son of Jamaican-born Christians and only converted to Islam a few years ago. These were fellow countrymen who in the name of God set out to slaughter their neighbours – a demonic twist in human affairs if ever there was one.

Perhaps the classical counterpart of Jesus' parable about the room swept clean of a single devil is the story of Pandora's Box. The great god Zeus gave Pandora the box as a wedding present with instructions that it was never to be opened. Her husband's curiosity got the better of him; he opened it and the evils that have afflicted the world ever since flew out. The only detail that might alleviate the gloom is that according to the myth, what came out of the box last was Hope.

Battle of Ideologies

Speaking the day after the London bombings, the Prime Minister said that the West 'must confront and defeat an evil ideology'. The widespread assumption is that the responsibility for combating this ideology rests with the Muslim communities, and certainly, only their scholars can refute the doctrinal claims of the suicide bombers. But what about the rest of society? What is our responsibility? We cannot just sit back and allow Muslims to battle it out. An ideology is a system of ideas that reflects the values of a nation or a group of people and also governs their lives. So how do we go about defeating an ideology? Security measures may contain it, restrict the activities of those who believe in it, but the key question is: What have we got to challenge it with? One ideology can only be countered by another more powerful or compelling.

The problem about combating the ideology of the suicide bombers is that our society has not much time for any ideology, good, bad or indifferent. Democratic socialism, which after decades of battling against capitalism eventually produced the first Labour government and the welfare state, is now so out of fashion that it dare not speak its name in government circles. The Tory party, in the throes of another leadership crisis, doesn't seem to be able to decide what Conservatism means in the twenty-first century. Communist ideology inspired perhaps the most extensive and ruthless experiment in social and political engineering in modern history, but it expired not because of outside opposition

so much as through the explosive pressures of the internal contradictions of the system. And Fascism, though persisting in some
Latin American republics and small racist groups in Britain, is no
longer a contender for world domination.

In Britain, the notion of people committing their whole life to
a set of beliefs, let alone being prepared to die for them, is alien to
the spirit of a society which lives by short-termism, which will try
this and that to see how things turn out, but which since the end
of Christendom has had no over-arching philosophy. Indeed, Al
Qa'eda has declared that there is a spiritual vacuum at the heart of
the materialistic West which it is determined to fill with its own
ideology.

Whole areas of the Church put less and less store on systems
of belief, which are felt to be difficult or divisive; there is a widespread conviction that it is not so much what Christians believe as
what they do that counts. The question, 'Does Christianity work?'
becomes the key question. Will it help to fight world poverty, keep
the crime figures down, strive for world peace, shore up the family? These are vitally important issues but there is a question still
more important. Søren Kierkegaard wrote, 'Christianity cannot
be a "to some extent" religion. Either it is true or it is not.'

This is the prior question, not 'Does Christianity work?' but 'Is
it true?' Does it render a profound account of the way the world
is and the way human nature is, and offer strategies for dealing
with them? For if Christianity is true, it changes everything. As
the playwright David Hare puts it, 'You will be forced totally to
reconstruct the model of the universe which you carry in your
head.' Just as the Tower of Babel crumbled when prodded by the
finger of God, so many a splendid system founded upon ideologi-
cal error has collapsed when challenged by the forces of history as
to its soundness rather than its efficiency or elegance.

Describing the clergymen he encountered while he was writing his play about the Church of England, *Racing Demon*,
David Hare praised them for their dedication and self-sacrifice

in serving their parishioners; but their principal fear, he said, was of what they called 'stuffing Christ down people's throats'. There was, he thought, material 'for a delightful comedy to come upon a Christian institution which seemed terrified of mentioning its own founder's name. A Labour Party which does not dare to use the word "socialism" is one thing, but a church which does not dare say "Christ" is quite another.'[1]

One might claim that the great dramatist is being a little over-dramatic about the state of the Church, but there is always the danger of Christianity being reduced to a combination of fervour and philanthropy. Christians also have the duty of contributing hard thinking to the life of our time, and where else could these distinctive explanations come from than the whole body of Christian doctrine?

Lest our faith hardens into that deadly certainty which in previous centuries had countless thousands of so-called heretics tortured and put to death for Christ's sake, it is necessary to register at this point that there are two important limits to the explanations offered by Christian doctrine. They explain a lot but they do not make the mistake of trying to explain everything. They observe a proper reticence about the strictly mysterious element in life, not what is as yet unknown until the big brains get around to unravelling it, but what will remain for ever unknowable – mystery not to be found beyond the present frontiers of knowledge but existing at the heart of the simplest things and everyday experiences. The Christian faith acknowledges that we are dealing with one who is beyond the range of our senses, who comes to meet us out of dazzling darkness, only if and when he chooses.

The other limit to Christian explanation is obvious. In the last resort neither individuals nor society can be saved by explanation, however profound. Intellectual assent to the truth of a doctrine is a very different thing from being converted by it; the former

---

1 David Hare, *Obedience, Struggle and Revolt*, Faber, 2005, p. 224.

requires mental readjustment whereas the latter needs a making and breaking of the human will. My natural mental powers might accomplish the one; only supernatural intervention can achieve the other.

If we didn't know it already, the events of 9/11 and what followed from them demonstrate the harsh truth that there is at work in our lives and in the world a deep corruption of the human will, which causes many of our problems and exacerbates the rest. It cannot be purged by the cunning application of the human mind, but only by a gospel of redemption whose source is in the being of God himself.

The new Pope, Benedict XVI, has insisted that the Christian creeds are a counter to the fads and fashions of the modern world. He has declared himself the enemy of all forms of short-termism and liberalism. He even believes the exercise of conscience is a sinful delusion if it does not harmonize with Church doctrine. In his homily to the conclave of cardinals in the Sistine Chapel before they retired to elect him Pope, Cardinal Ratzinger, as he was then, urged, 'Having a clear faith, based on the creed of the Church is often labelled fundamentalism, whereas relativism, which is letting oneself be tossed or swept along by every wind of teaching, looks like the only attitude acceptable by today's standards.'

Thus, he highlights the other temptation of the modern Church, to sit lightly to Christian doctrine compared to a touchy-feely kind of personal experience. The words of Jesus to the woman of Samaria strike uncomfortably close to home, 'You worship what you do not know' (John 4.22). The balance between belief and experience has swung so decisively that many Christians seem to believe more and more fervently in less and less.

The rich Christology of the creeds has shrunk to the bare convictions needed to support a Jesus cult. Classical hymnody, rich in doctrine, is losing out to pious jingles, mesmeric in their repetitiveness, of a banality which demeans both the deity and the English language. Of course, Protestants pride themselves that theirs is an experiential faith. They echo the words of Charles Wesley's hymn, 'My God, I know, I feel thee mine!', but the next line runs, 'Steadfast by faith I stand.' Who can doubt that the faith by which he stood was that of the holy catholic and apostolic Church? Personal experience unless illuminated by doctrine is just raw fervour and can mean anything or nothing. Belief is an emotion triggered by an idea, but if the idea is trivial then the emotion is little more than a glandular tic.

When I ponder the issue really deeply, I realize that my own religious experience has been decisively shaped by the theology I have brought to it rather than by any religious truth I discovered there. For example, I have no internal spiritual apparatus fine-tuned enough to detect and distinguish between individual Persons of the Trinity. Why would it even cross my mind there could be a trinitarian deity unless someone put the idea into my head? I might have some general sense of God's presence, but what kind of evidence would show that he is in fact three Persons in one God? After all, if unaided I could detect the presence in my life of three distinct beings of God, why stop there? Perhaps if I look hard enough, I might stretch it to a dozen.

All my life can be explained on the supposition that Christianity is true. I can see lucky accidents as providential, the path I have chosen as a vocation and the strength to resist my besetting temptations as continuous gifts of grace. Those moments when prayer has come easily, I say God is close, and when he seems more distant then I declare it a time of testing. But in thinking like this I am making a number of theological assumptions about the meaning of my experience. I could find other explanations (genetic, environmental, psychological) for the course my life has taken without invoking God or religion at all. From my experience alone, I cannot settle the truth of Christianity one way or the other. I have no way of proving that a non-religious explanation of my life is wrong: I have seen no blinding lights and heard no heavenly voices.

Some Christians claim that there are supernatural evidences within human experience which prove religious dogmas – statues weeping, stigmata on the hands of saints, ecstatic visions, miraculous healings and a whole host of minor miracles. Yet it is only because the authorities who investigate these miracles are already Christian that they attribute them to Jesus Christ or the Virgin Mary. If they were not, they might nominate Allah or Zeus or whatever other supernatural agency they believe is behind the world. There are records of stigmata in the Sufi Islamic tradition, the eyes of statues of the Buddha have been known to weep, Hindu holy men accomplish extraordinary feats, and even some New Age gurus claim to heal the sick.

Believers accept these special experiences as proof of their own religion's truth because they have decided beforehand *who to give the credit to.* The proof lies not in the experience itself but in the minds of those who interpret it. Indeed, the credit need not be given to any deity at all. Didn't Jesus warn his disciples that the Devil disguises himself as an angel of light? The case of Joan of Arc is illuminating. The English claimed she was a witch; the French said that she was a saint. Both explanations suited the facts.

The point is: none of these factions can prove from personal experience that those who hold different views are in error. They can bombard each other with scriptural texts and pray in aid great doctors and saints of the Church, but they cannot say, for example, 'My personal experience proves that Christ is the only way to salvation.' They may have discovered that he is the only way for them, but if they are going to use personal experience as the acid test, they cannot discount the experience of millions of religious devotees who claim to have found other ways to salvation.

No Christian doctrine can be proved from personal experience alone. Take God's providential rule over the world. It could equally well be argued that the world is controlled by a malevolent spirit who shows his true nature in drought, cancer cell, concentration camp and war, untimely death and human misery, who rejoices in screams of agony, who created human beings with a complicated nervous system in order that they might be capable of exquisite suffering, and has decreed that despite the billions of years of evolutionary pain which went into their making, humans shall live for a mere instant and then vanish for ever.

This theory accords with much human observation and experience; I certainly cannot disprove it. Why then do I find it intolerable? It has nothing to do with the weight of evidence for and against, but it has everything to do with this strange obsession in my mind, which I call faith and which impels me to judge evil in terms of good and not good in terms of evil. I am making a prior assumption in the light of which I judge everything else. I have resolved to consider evil an invader in a good world rather than the driving force of a bad world shot through with bursts of goodness. And I find any other explanation literally unthinkable – though that isn't scientific evidence, for I may be completely deluded; my mental processes in a hopeless tangle.

Some years ago I did a series of radio talks, later turned into a book called *Starting from Scratch*, in which I tried to see how far along the road to Christian faith I could get using only my common sense. I came to a shuddering full stop after I had discussed spiritual penny-dropping experiences and the calamitous effects of my pride placing me at the centre of my universe. I just ran out of common sense explanations. Where did I go next? The story of Jesus of Nazareth inspired, his teaching enlightened and his death was utterly tragic, but to bridge the gap from the historic Jesus to Paul's great summary of the rock-bottom minimal Christian creed – 'God was in Christ reconciling the world to himself' (2 Corinthians 5.19, RSV) – was impossible. I couldn't put a wet towel round my head and think my way to that.

In Paul's declaration I was confronted by a dogma, in its simplest meaning, a religious truth established by divine revelation and defined by the Church. There is this take-it-or-leave-it aspect to great Christian doctrines. The evidence in Bible and tradition is never beyond argument, otherwise the early Church would not have squabbled over it for centuries. I needed to make a leap of faith. And that faith could only be a divine gift, because I could not account for it in any other way. It enabled me to approach a historic Christian doctrine echoing the ancient words, 'O my God, I believe this, because thou hast taught it me.' Faith is an act of God's creative self-revelation which awakens in me a deep need I never knew I possessed and it is met by the revealed truth of the gospel, expressed in a series of doctrines which together point the way to salvation.

To argue strongly in defence of doctrine in a sceptical age is to invite a charge of bigotry, especially when ecumenicity invites us to be open to truths that are not our own. But this accusation misunderstands the nature of bigotry. Bigotry is the anger of those who have no true convictions, only prejudices; it is the frenzy of the doctrinally indifferent. Bigotry is an unholy alliance of passion and ignorance, not a wholesome marriage of passion and truth.

Which takes us back by a circuitous route to suicide bombers. The London bombers have been described in the press as cowardly or mad. They were neither craven nor lunatics. They were men of faith who set about dying and killing for what they believed, however repellent most normal people would find those beliefs. The Prime Minister was right to recognize that we face a deadly ideology. The bombers were doctrinaire about their religion to the last dot and comma.

So the Christian contribution to this battle of ideologies, besides owning up to the strands of intolerance and violence in our own tradition, is to offer a faith that by its breadth rules out fanaticism, is sharp enough to bring to bear a critical intelligence on those political policies which are contentious matters at the present time, and is deep enough to sustain a life-long commitment, delivering us from hysteria or despair.

Part Two – 9/11

The Day that Changed the World

11 September 2001, the day on which terrorists attacked the Twin
Towers in New York and the Pentagon in Washington, has joined
the eleventh day of the eleventh month of 1918, when the First
World War ended, or 3 September 1939 when the Second World
War began as dates that demand commemoration. It has been described as the day that changed the world for ever. Consider what
Osama bin Laden did when his followers attacked the United
States. He caused President Bush to declare war on international
terrorism and to invade both Afghanistan and Iraq. He has bitterly
divided the United Nations, forced a split in the European Union
and brought an already overheated Middle East to boiling point.
He has made the British government restrict civil liberties, some
of which had been on the statute book for 800 years; he sent stock
markets spiralling, increased the cost and delays of international
travel and inspired terrorist alerts almost every day somewhere
in the world. He has been responsible for Muslim minorities in
Western countries being regarded with suspicion and therefore
put strains on community relations. And the death toll steadily
mounts, culminating in the London bombings on another day
that will be permanently marked in the calendars.

The philosopher John Gray has written that the suicide
bombers, besides killing thousands of civilians, also destroyed
the myth that in the modern world, war means conflict between

states; if there were to be any more wars they would be affairs of armies and governments. The received wisdom was that in the nuclear age, the best way to avoid such catastrophic clashes would be to strengthen international organizations such as the United Nations and the international courts of justice. In any case, the increasing interdependence of the global economy would have as one of its benefits the realization that modern states cannot afford to disrupt world trade by going to war.

Al Qa'eda destroyed these assumptions. It is an international organization but owes allegiance to no state, it is not fighting on behalf of any, not even the countries that give it shelter. One of the great fears of the West, that Al Qa'eda might get hold of nuclear weapons, is not simply because that could multiply its destructive capacity; it would make nonsense of the whole concept of nuclear deterence, which is based on mutual assured destruction – your homeland would be laid waste in retaliation for a nuclear strike against mine. Al Qa'eda has no homeland, no capital city, no military installations, no identifiable targets.

Al Qa'eda claims its chief enemy is the American Empire which in conquering the world has created a spiritual vacuum that must be filled with radical Islam. In one sense Al Qa'eda is a throwback to medieval times when wars of religion were the norm, but it uses the most modern technology and recruits clever and well-educated Muslims as its warriors. It doesn't represent a revolt of the masses; it has more in common with some of the nineteenth-century anarchist movements which were largely made up of intellectuals.

All these consequences flowed from 11 September. The world of the West certainly changed on that day, but it is not the only world. Many Latin Americans recall the date for a different reason. On 11 September 1973 President Pinochet of Chile began a campaign against political opponents that left thousands dead or in prison. Or take another key date, 8 April 1994. This was the day the genocide began in Rwanda and over a million Tutsis were slaughtered. That day hardly changed our world; it should have done, but it didn't. Europe and America hardly noticed what was happening far away in the wilds of Central Africa.

It is understandable that the victims of an appalling atrocity should feel their suffering and anger are central to the concerns of the whole globe, especially if their wealth and power have hitherto made them assume that they were invulnerable. But it is a religious insight that beyond a certain point, to put ourselves and our interests at the centre of things and expect the rest of humanity to arrange itself around us distorts our view of reality.

So universal is this human tendency towards personal and national self-regard that to correct it another date is crucial. In all the Christian creeds, there is only one day mentioned, a single time reference. This is when the Apostles' Creed says that Jesus 'was crucified under Pontius Pilate'. The intention was not to vilify a minor Roman official but to anchor who Jesus was and what he did firmly within the same history as all the other events whose dates we commemorate.

To detect the drift of history when great forces are at work as in the present crisis about international terrorism, one needs an absolute vantage point within and yet beyond history. Paul insists that the cross provides that. It puts catastrophe in its true perspective, for the God who did not spare his own Son will not scruple to bend the most dreadful eventualities to his purposes. The Christian contention is that this was the world's supreme crisis, beyond any imaginable human disaster. The future can add nothing in principle to the great settlement of good and evil made on Calvary. There is nothing ahead of humanity that has not already been discounted there.

It was P. T. Forsyth who said that the cross was the pivot on which not just Christianity but the world turned. He thought the theologians of the Reformation were right and the creed makers were wrong. The Reformers put the cross where the New Testament puts it – at the centre; the creed makers mention it only in passing. 'A holy God, self-atoned in Christ, is the moral centre of the sinful world,' he wrote. Thus, the world's ultimate crisis doesn't loom ahead at some future date as predicted by religious or secular prophets of doom; it is already behind us. It did not happen on 11 September 2001, terrible as that day was. It was another day, way, way back, that changed the world for ever.

President Bush's Bible Class

After the attacks on the Twin Towers and the Pentagon on 11 September 2001, President Bush, a devout Methodist evangelical, unapologetically expressed in theological terms his initial response to the atrocities, declaring, 'We are in a conflict between good and evil, and America will call evil by its name.' In the same vein, a year later he proclaimed North Korea, Iran and Iraq to be an 'axis of evil'; he talked often of the 'evil ones' and occasionally of 'the servants of evil'. According to the philosopher Peter Singer, President Bush has spoken about evil in over 300 separate speeches. And he uses the term not only as an adjective to describe demonic human behaviour, but as a noun – he sees evil as a force that has real existence in the world. By contrast, he declared the United States to be 'a moral nation' and assured the American people that 'good will come out of evil'.

This made sense to Mr Garry Walby, a retired jeweller from Florida who at a Bush election rally was reported by the *New York Times* as declaring that at last he knew where God was. He said, 'For the first time I feel God is in the White House.' The rapturous audience at the rally roared their approval, obviously seeing in their mind's eye God standing at the President's right hand in the Operations Room at the White House directing the campaign against the legions of hell.

Obviously, there is another 'Operations Room' at the White House from which the spiritual wing of the Crusade against Evil (the President's description) functions. A Bible group established by George Bush when he was first elected President meets regularly in the Eisenhower Executive Office. The Attorney General, John Ashcroft, also holds daily Bible studies at the Justice Department. Attendance, said one of the President's aides, is not compulsory but it's not exactly voluntary either. Clearly, the President takes the study of the Scriptures very seriously.

George Bush is not the first President to encourage religious activities at the White House. Jimmy Carter, a Baptist, taught adult Sunday school, and the Quaker, Richard Nixon, regularly invited evangelists to address his staff. But George Bush has publicly announced that prayer and Bible study will be a priority in his presidency; they will govern his life and witness as the most powerful leader in the Western world.

So, what might the Bible be saying to the group as it seeks divine guidance in the 'war against terror'? For example, in the week prior to 25 December, when the White House was dominated by a gigantic Christmas tree and local church choirs took turns singing carols in the main lobby, the Bible group, if they were following the lectionary, would have reached the chapter of Luke's Gospel which includes that verse we call the Magnificat, 'He has brought down the powerful from their thrones, and has lifted up the lowly; he has filled the hungry with good things, and sent the rich away empty' (Luke 1.52–3). I wonder what they made of that as they sat at the heart of the mightiest power on earth?

Given our capacity for deluding ourselves (one more evidence of evil's power to distort our thinking) when the Bible group read of God 'bringing down the powerful from their thrones', they would no doubt have in mind Saddam Hussein and the other leaders of the 'axis of evil'. The idea that a superpower much closer to home might fit the bill probably never occurred to them.

The problem is that in pin-pointing the enemy as 'international terrorism', the President has effectively declared war on an abstraction; it is a category error that obscures the deeper causes of the problem. It also means it will be a war without end, just as the 'wars' on crime and poverty are: they have been raging for as long as anyone can remember. 'Terrorism' is like one of those mythical monsters; if you cut off a dozen of its tentacles another hundred will immediately sprout to replace them. The British Prime Minister does not believe that. He shares President Bush's confidence that the war on terrorism can be won. He has said, 'We will not rest until this evil is driven from our world.' This is the Pelagian heresy in modern dress. Pelagius, a fourth-century Celt, believed in human perfectability and disputed St Augustine's contention that evil is an intrinsic part of human nature.

The 'Manual of Spiritual Warfare', as one of the White House group members quaintly describes the Bible, demolishes any confident declaration that a great evil can be finally banished from the world. Jesus tells a story about wheat and weeds (good and evil) growing together in a field, nourished by the same sun, often indistinguishable and always inseparable until they are cut down at harvest time (Matthew 13.24–30). History is not a success story – a saga of the irresistible onward march of goodness and the inexorable pushing back of evil. Far from evil being systematically eradicated as time wears on, even at the eleventh hour, it will make a last bid to frustrate God's purposes.

Evil must be fought but it cannot be destroyed by any political strategy whether based on overwhelming military force, tougher security laws or the spread of democratic values. The New Testament says that only a decisive divine intervention, what Jesus calls the harvest, can do that. Even President Bush's 'moral nation' cannot win this war because its policies and actions are inevitably tainted by and therefore spread the very evil it is trying to get rid of. Thus the war on terrorism kills the innocent as well as the guilty, and it is not just Saddam's butchers but also coalition soldiers who abuse prisoners. The technology on which much of the West's dominance has been built is employed on the one side to lay waste to Iraqi cities like Fallujah, and on the other, it is exploited by the insurgents – apparently, the mobile phone is an essential weapon they use to alert car bombers to the approach of targets.

But the Bible group will also be confronting another central theme of the Old Testament. They will look in vain to find scriptural backing for President Bush's insistence that God is supporting the West's crusade against terror. If the Old Testament is to be believed, God is against all superpowers because as the largest concentrations of earthly might, in their pride and arrogance they become idolatrous, claiming God-like authority for their values, imposing their way of life on nations weaker than themselves, especially those of the little people of the earth who are God's particular concern.

The collapse of the Soviet Union gave the United States the illusion of omnipotence as the world's only superpower. Its troops are now stationed in 120 countries and it controls or influences the policies of many other nations because of its overwhelming economic strength. And if international law or conventions stand in its way, it reserves the right to act unilaterally in defence of its interests.

This is not to suggest that the American people are more venal than any other. Many of them have a strong social conscience, they care for the poor and desire a just society. They are naturally generous in spirit, and the range of their religious convictions reflects the size of their country and the diversity of its culture. Hard-line fundamentalists are a significant minority, but many Christians are ecumenical in temper and are anxious to understand and co-operate with devotees of other faiths.

Nevertheless, the US believes its form of government is the best in the world and it has the right to export it to any other country. Sadly it fits the biblical profile of an idolatrous nation. Its virtues are no excuse. Even the most righteous nation found itself in the dock. Go further back in the Bible and there is the paradoxical word God speaks as he surveys the Tower of Babel, that monument to humanity's first attempt to flex its muscles and take over heaven. 'You have done well. Therefore I will bring your efforts to nothing!'

The Old Testament is an epic chronicle of the rise and fall of superpowers – the Egyptians, the Assyrians, the Chaldeans, the Medes and Persians – all glorying in their achievements, militarily irresistible, boasting in the righteousness of their cause and the superiority of their way of life. One after another they are brought low, either with God's active co-operation or with his approval.

So the Bible group will have to come to terms with the fact that the moral triumphalism of the world's only superpower as articulated by President Bush is dangerously unbiblical. Granted, in the aftermath of 9/11, there were dissenting voices from the general clamour of righteous rhetoric in America proclaiming the nation's virtue and calling for fearsome retribution upon evil. Curiously, two of these voices belonged to fundamentalist television evangelists with millions of followers, Gerry Falwell and Pat Robertson. They certainly enthusiastically supported massive retribution against evil, and they knew exactly what its source was – 'Islam is a religion that seeks to dominate and then destroy us,' declared Pat Robertson – but God's Own Country must first put its affairs in order. They said that God was not standing shoulder to shoulder with the American people but towering over them in righteous wrath. The terrorist attacks were a divine punishment for the sinfulness of the American people.

On Pat Robertson's TV show, 'The 700 Club', Dr Falwell declared: 'I really believe that the pagans and abortionists and the feminists and the gays and lesbians – all of them have tried to secularize America. I put a finger in their face and say, "You helped this to happen." ' The Revd Fred Phelps, a Baptist minister from Topika, Kansas concurred. Protesting at the consecration of gay bishop Gene Robinson, he shouted out, 'September 11 2001 was a very good day. It was God's judgement on a sinful, faggot-ridden, fornicating nation. It was a sign.'

There was a biblical ring to such prophetic denunciations, though the specific targets owed more to bigotry than to holy writ. In the Old Testament it was clearly not the particular sexual habits of a nation's citizens so much as the state's God-like pretensions that attracted divine judgement. There are stretches of the Bible that record the blood-thirsty nature of this judgement. God allows whole communities to be massacred or he massacres them himself through plagues, fire from heaven and other enormities. On one occasion, an angry God gives David a stern choice – either three years of famine or three days of the sword of the Lord. David made his choice, 'so the Lord sent a pestilence on Israel . . . and seventy thousand of the people died' (2 Samuel 24.15).

Unlike theological liberals who do not believe literally in the record of a vengeful God but judge the lowest expressions of divinity in the Bible by the highest, we are told that the members of the White House Bible group believe the Scriptures to be the inspired word of God, which must include these grisly incidents where a wrathful God lays low his human enemies. Because of their veneration for Scripture, President Bush, his Bible class and the neo-cons who support him must take these accounts of God's judgement upon earthly empires with the utmost seriousness. How can they avoid the conclusion that the West is more likely to be on the receiving end of God's judgement than to gain his approval for a holy war?

The Fall of the Tower of Babel

A couple of days after the terrorist attacks on the Eastern sea-board of the United States, I was due to contribute to *Thought for the Day* on Radio 4. As I watched those apocalyptic television images of the World Trade Towers crashing in a hellish vision of fire and dust, the biblical image that came irresistibly to mind was the description in the Bible about the collapse of the Tower of Babel. But with thousands dying before our eyes and countless more suffering irreparable loss, it would have been both cruel and tasteless to confront a wounded society with the harsh moral of the story of Babel. The Bible offers words of hope and faith, of consolation and courage, and they needed to be heard in the days following the atrocity.

But the time for mourning has passed and the myth of Babel still looms out of the distant past to cast its shadow over the post-9/11 world. It is the story of a jealous God who punishes human beings for their arrogance in presuming to raise monuments to their greatness high enough to abolish the gulf between earth and heaven.

Every civilization marks its great achievements by tangible symbols, like the Union Flag on the summit of Everest or the Stars and Stripes on the surface of the moon. The key-notes of Western civilization have been Faster! Higher! Bigger! Stronger! Richer! More! And so intoxicated have we become with our virtuosity and efficiency that we have forgotten the harsh threefold moral the myth of Babel teaches: we are mere mortals – that is our fate; we refuse to accept our mortality – that is our sin; we are brought low – that is our punishment.

And our gravest sins are more likely to be the by-product of our greatest achievements than our most bestial acts, which is why Babel takes the form of a tower rather than a trench.

It would be foolish to single out the United States or the West alone for condemnation. Every culture raises its Tower of Babel. Babels literally thrust heavenwards not just in New York but throughout the world – in Malaysia which boasts the highest building on earth or Saudi Arabia with its breathtaking two new chrome and concrete hotels shaped like galleons in full sail. And further east, a forest of commercial tower blocks dominate the skyline in nations as ideologically opposed as Singapore and China. All are awesome symbols of irresistible power in the modern world.

But sooner or later, these monuments to our greatness become memorials to the death of what we are celebrating. The Egyptian pyramids were barely completed before the civilization they glorified had perished. The Justinian Code was the epitome of the grandeur of the Roman law, but by the time it was expressed in final form, the Roman Empire was in ruins. And it was a strange coincidence that what was then the tallest building in the world, the Empire State Building in New York, proud symbol of the glories of capitalism, was completed in the same year the great depression devastated the American economy, so that its hundreds of floors stayed empty for years. And the paint was barely dry on the spanking new League of Nations building in Geneva when Mussolini tore up the Charter, invaded Abyssinia and reduced the world organization to impotence.

There is actually some humour in the story of Babel. Humans busily build their tower, bigger and higher than anything ever seen on earth, happily believing they are getting nearer to their goal of dispossessing God from his heavenly home. Then God says, 'What's going on down there?' The narrative suggests he has to peer very closely because the Tower of Babel, so colossal when viewed from the ground, is almost invisible from heaven.

God pokes the tower with his finger and it crashes to earth. There is something almost contemptuous about that casual gesture. But take the old story out of the realms of mythology, accept its truth and ask the Bible how God's judgement against our Towers of Babel operates within history. Sometimes it happens by simply allowing things to take their course.

According to Jeremiah (2.19), God says, 'Your wickedness will punish you, and your apostasies will convict you.' Disaster results from God's non-intervention. There are some terrible words in Paul's Letter to the Romans. Writing about one group of people, he comments, 'For this reason God gave them up' (Romans 1.26). He didn't hurl thunderbolts at them or strike them down, he merely left them to their own devices.

One of the most disturbing stories in the Gospels is that of the healing of the ten lepers (Luke 17.11–19). Jesus heals all ten, but only one, a Samaritan, returns to thank him. The other nine go their way and resume their old life. The interesting question is: why did Jesus accept the situation without protest or complaint? Why didn't he call the nine back and remonstrate with them, pointing out what a miracle had been done for them and how they were insulting God by their ingratitude? He leaves it at that, accepting their verdict. The moral is that if we are unmoved by God, the danger is not that in his anger he may consume us but that he may accept his failure with us without protest. He just lets things take their course. He confronts us, we make our choice, and in judging him we are judged.

Politically, what are the implications of God doing nothing? It means allowing the internal contradictions of our earthly systems to bring them crashing. This is what happened to the Eastern bloc. During the cold war, the West carried on a relentless struggle, just short of actual hostilities, against Communism. But in the end, the Soviet Empire disintegrated not through an external military threat but because of its internal contradictions; the relentless repression of the human spirit finally produced explosive forces that could no longer be contained. The whole machine shuddered to a halt, expiring not with a bang but a whimper.

Nor is the West without its internal contradictions, the pressures created by vast inequalities of wealth and power in a world whose resources are finite and population growing; our spoliation of the environment, our relentless pursuit of self-interest. The submissiveness of the poor of the earth is giving way to a terrible anger and resentment. 'How can they hate us so much?' asked an American in anguish, observing the ruins of the Twin Towers.

When God chooses to act rather than allowing things to take their course, he uses two forces, his agents and his instruments. God's agents are those who respond to his call, seek first his kingdom and find their highest ends in fulfilling his – initially a chosen people, then when they lost their way, one Jew, Jesus, who utterly identified himself with the divine will. First, a people, then a man, then another people as disciples responded to his call because they saw the light of the glory of God in his face. They became agents of God as the one, holy, catholic and apostolic Church.

But God's instruments, who are they? I suppose the short answer is: anybody his eye lights upon; who happens to be in the right place at the right time. All humans are potentially God's instruments. Nothing they can do or think or plan will prevent God using them. When their wisdom fails, their foolishness still serves him; their wrath praises him when their obedience falters, their treachery vindicates his holiness; he builds on the ruins of their ambitions and hopes. This is the lesson of the cross, God bending and moulding the most dreadful eventualities as the instruments of his purpose.

That is how God's judgement works in history. If God cannot find agents, he will use instruments; if there are no volunteers, he will employ conscripts. He tells Jeremiah to run to and fro through the streets of Jerusalem, saying, 'See if you can find one person' (Jeremiah 5.1). And when the prophet fails to find a human agent, God employs a terrifying instrument: utter calamity.

The story of the Tower of Babel describes a human condition totally without hope. If it stood alone in the Bible without a sequel, humanity could only be resigned to its fate. But it was at Pentecost that the curse of Babel was cancelled. Humanity found a new centre on which it could cohere, reconciled and transformed. The infinite distance between God and humanity which Babel failed to bridge had been spanned in and through Jesus. All present began to speak in a common language for the first time since the dawn of history when, according to Genesis, humans settled in the land of Shinar and conspired together to depose God. This new language, which transcends all the old linguistic differences, is the language of benediction, causing the Lord's name to be praised.

And out of Pentecost emerged not just a common language but a society without frontiers, the New Israel, whose citizens are drawn from every corner of the earth, and unlike those of earthly nations are called and chosen rather than thrown together by biological accident. The Christ who is hidden within the world is manifest and reigns over a New Israel. And whereas the nations of the world are agglomerations of great power, the New Israel glories in its powerlessness, choosing suffering rather than self-assertion as its key-signature. By the power of the Spirit, the New Israel presents a living picture of what corporate redemption could mean, for it is not made of different stuff from the rest of the world; it *is* that part of the world shot through with the regenerative power of God.

And the conflicts of colour, race and class which are resolved by compromise within the nations are transcended in the New Israel by reconciliation, the destruction of all particularities through and in Jesus Christ. Within the nation, the New Israel testifies to

God's rule by the proclamation of Christ's lordship, by the office of intercession and by a quality of witness which is a steadfast refusal to allow divine commands to take second place to those of the state; a witness which reminds the nation that its primary engagement is with God.

From Babel to Pentecost is a long, long journey – 1,100 pages in my Bible – yet it can be accomplished in the twinkling of an eye, the time it takes for humans to realize that not even the greatest achievements of their societies can bridge the gulf between earth and heaven. But seen close up, the chasm is an optical illusion. Jesus has not merely spanned it but closed it for all time: there is a Man in Heaven. Is there not aptness in this image of the triumph of the horny-handed workman of Nazareth who would be more at home filling in trenches than erecting towers?

The Christian as Assassin

There was modified rapture when Saddam Hussein was captured, found unkempt and hungry, huddled in a hole in the ground, his whereabouts betrayed by one of his generals for 10 million US dollars. Every spokesman who commented on the arrest – President, Prime Minister and US administrator – went to great lengths to emphasize that Saddam would get a fair trial; he would have access to lawyers, with no expense spared to see him treated justly.

This is in jarring contrast to the fate of thousands of unnamed people throughout the world who are being held under anti-terrorist legislation. They do not know what the evidence against them is or when they might be freed. Unlike Saddam Hussein they are unlikely to enjoy the luxury of defending themselves in a public trial.

Some of them may be guilty of planning terrorist attacks, in which case, the courts should deal with them as they will deal with Saddam; but by the law of averages, some of these prisoners will be innocent, victims of mistaken identity, bureaucratic muddle or informers paying off old scores.

It must be terrifying to be beyond the reach of the normal processes of law, in a legal limbo where your fate is decided for reasons shrouded in mystery. It is ironic that if your crimes, like Saddam Hussein's, scream to high heaven for retribution, you will benefit from the due process of law, but if someone has reason to believe you are implicated in terrorist activities not remotely on the same scale, theoretically, you can lie in gaol until you rot.

No doubt the government would say that it is to protect our way of life that they enacted the anti-terrorist legislation passed a couple of years ago, and now intend to add to its clauses following the London bombings. But to use the law to put someone beyond the reach of the courts is to raise not just moral but religious issues. Edmund Burke in his *Letter to the Sheriffs of Bristol* wrote, 'There is only one law, the law that governs all law, the law of our Creator.' It is a biblical insight that the law which rules our daily lives is an imperfect manifestation of the law of God which is the ultimate source of its authority. No human being, not even Saddam Hussein, is outside God's law, but then, neither is anyone else, including unnamed detainees in our special prisons.

But another equally troubling moral issue was raised by the capture of Saddam Hussein. An American military spokesman said that it took so long to neutralize Saddam Hussein because attempts to assassinate him, to 'cut off the head of the beast' as he put it, had failed. The first attempt was made before the war began with an air missile attack on a house in Baghdad where a party was being held at which, according to an informer, Saddam was supposed to be a guest. The informer was wrong, and a number of innocent Iraqis died. But the spokesman went on to say that a secret Special Forces US unit had been operating in Iraq for some time, trying to target Saddam Hussein and assassinate him.

We are referring here to the lawful ruler of a sovereign state. Western public opinion would view with utter abhorrence any Al Qa'eda boasts about their attempts to assassinate President Bush or Prime Minister Blair, but apparently we were prepared to act as judge, jury and executioner on the Iraqi leader.

The United States is a very religious country and its armed forces no doubt reflect the fact. It is unlikely that the Pentagon recruited only atheists to form their special assassination unit, so there must be some Christians in it. How did they reconcile the mission with their faith? I suppose they could cite Dietrich Bonhoeffer in their defence since he was the most distinguished Christian would-be assassin of modern times. And there are some important and topical morals to be drawn from his witness.

Christians are moved and inspired by the story of Bonhoeffer's defiant death at the hands of the Flossenberg Prison hangman in 1945, but the tougher truth is that he was a justly condemned accessory to murder. In fact, a number of those implicated in the plot to kill Hitler were Christian gentlemen. Their last words and poise in the presence of death leave no room for doubt about that. The plot failed, and its timing raises troubling questions about Christian motives. I exclude Christian pacifists from this argument because they will never take life, even in the face of un-doubted evil. They would be prepared to die but not to kill; for them it is 'the more excellent way' of love unto death or nothing.

Even those Christians who will take up arms usually cannot bring themselves to use violence to destroy evil until it is in full flower. Yet the same blow, struck while that evil was still a furtive thing of the back streets, might have benefited millions of future victims of Hitler's homicidal mania. If the plotters against Hitler had struck ten years earlier, before the smoke of the gas cham-bers blackened the sky and Europe's cities were aflame, or had the Allies been prepared to give more support to the German resistance movement, who knows how history might have been changed?

That is the cheap wisdom of hindsight, of course, but there is a grievous dilemma here for the Christian. In 1934 Hitler, far from being castigated as a loathsome tyrant, was widely acclaimed both within Germany and outside as a dynamic, enlightened ruler carv-ing a great nation out of the rubble of the First World War. To have killed him at that time would have reserved for Bonhoeffer and his fellow conspirators a place of infamy alongside Lee Harvey Oswald who killed J. F. Kennedy. If Christians can only be sure that they are right to use violence when evil screams its true nature to the world, they will invariably strike too late. If, on the other hand, they cut down the poisonous bloom while it is still a weak shoot, how can they be sure that they have plucked weed and not wheat?

What would Jesus have done? I am sure that is a question any Christian members of the US Special Forces must have asked themselves. How can cold-blooded assassination be reconciled with Jesus' teaching, the recurrent theme of which was the law of love as the supreme standard of human life?

A casual reading of the parables of Jesus rules out of court any suggestion that he was a dewy-eyed sentimentalist who went on about love because the harsher side of life was a closed book to him. In his teaching, he drew many of his illustrations from the area of society where people contend for power and speak the language of violence. In one place he talks of a king who orders those who will not accept his rule to be put to death; somewhere else he describes another king who, in anger, razed a city to the ground. He used the images of robbers binding strong men and attacking travellers; some of his subjects were crooked agents, tough businessmen and domineering slave owners.

Jesus was no lotus-eater, shutting his eyes and mind to the tough and unpleasant aspects of life. And this sharpens the dilemma. Knowing the ways of the world, he still said that we should love our enemies, turn the other cheek when provoked and forgive with monotonous regularity. This issue has to be faced head-on whenever we contemplate violence or actually go to war. The love ethic of Jesus is absolute, and its motivation seems entirely religious rather than a matter of political practicality – we ought to forgive because God forgives us; we should love indiscriminately because that is how the grace of God operates.

Any social order based literally on the teaching of Jesus would be hopelessly impractical: perfect love removing the need for the compulsions of the law, the checks on power, the administrations of justice? And where love is perfect, all distinctions between what is our own and someone else's would disappear. As Reinhold Niebuhr, the theologian who thought most deeply about political problems in the twentieth century, put it: 'The social ideal of Jesus is as perfect and as impossible of attainment as his personal ideal.'

Yet if Jesus was human at all – and the Letter to the Hebrews insists that 'he has been tested in every respect as we are' (Hebrews 4.15) – he was a political being, living within social structures protected from chaos by the use of power. Those who say that Jesus kept aloof from specific political issues in loyalty to a higher destiny must recognize that by doing so, he was making a political decision with profound implications. Politics is about power; how it is used, and to what end. Those who decide, for whatever reason, that they will not touch power, are abdicating to others the right to decide how it will be used. This is a political judgement and they cannot evade some share of the responsibility if unscrupulous people use that power destructively.

This is a dilemma on which all Christians, whether soldiers or civilians, are impaled. We can strive to make the love ethic which Jesus commends the law of our being, but we cannot seek to impose it on the state or a political party or any larger group, because as institutions they can neither give nor receive love. The individual Christian can choose to the follow the cross, the way of love unto death, but it must be *freely* chosen; it cannot be forced on someone without their consent. This is why the cross could never become the core of a political philosophy, because the state exists for purposes which are the precise opposite of the way of love unto death. Its role is to preserve life, to shield its members from extinction, whether by threat of outside enemies, internal chaos or natural hazard. And if it is a democracy it is entitled to use compulsion to get the obedience of its citizens; a majority of the citizens have the right to compel a minority to observe its laws. The state cannot choose the way of love unto death without denying the basic reasons for its existence. (Hmm.....

The truth is that the love ethic in its pure form cannot come to terms with the compulsion which is a necessary feature of all organized life. Followed through to its limit, the love ethic would deny Christians any participation in political life at all because they will seek in vain for a system pure enough to deserve their devotion.

Every time Christians go to war or use force for what they believe are righteous ends, they are required to wrestle with and reject the impossible demands of Jesus. Christian pacifists, like those who embrace the monastic life or choose to be celibate, are testifying to the perfect law of the kingdom, but they are not without their own dilemmas; chiefly, how can they be politically relevant without endorsing the compulsive power of the state?

Christian pacifists and non-pacifists alike are 'united in the fellowship of suffering and the solidarity of guilt' – that was the phrase used by the German Church at the time of Hitler to unite those who felt that Hitler must be overthrown if necessary by assassination and those who believed that such an option was not open to the Christian. This is not a debate either side can win. There are no easy solutions, just common anguish.

'The Gloves Are Off!'

Sometimes a casual remark can cast unexpected light on a dark subject. During the Iraq War it was reported that a suspected terrorist had been captured in Saudi Arabia, whether by the Saudis or the Americans wasn't made clear, but the reporter commented that the Americans would probably leave him in Saudi hands because they would put more pressure on him to reveal all he knew. That sounded ominous. Since 9/11, the Americans in their righteous anger have not been shy of revealing the robustness with which they interrogate prisoners – 'stress and duress' is the official term, which includes sleep deprivation, being forced to stand for hours in one position without moving, blindfolds and ear muffs to shut out all the sights and sounds of normality, and the use of drugs. The head of the Central Intelligence Agency's counter-terrorist unit, Cofer Black, told the US Congress, 'There was a before and after 9/11. After 9/11, the gloves have come off.' If all that is permissible under American control, what could be the greater pressure the Saudi government might apply?

A common view was that these people deserved all they got, even though they were held beyond the reach of the law, their families and the humanitarian agencies. According to one press report, it is estimated that over 12,000 people throughout the world have been branded as terrorists and are detained without trial. The moral justification is that robust interrogation yields intelligence to foil further terrorist attacks. But if any of these prisoners should be innocent, what can they reveal that will cause their captors to cease tormenting them?

It will be dismissed as bleeding-heart liberalism to be concerned about the fate of alleged terrorist prisoners when appalling atrocities are being suffered daily at the hands of suicide bombers. But Jesus did say that whatever we do to the prisoner, we do to him. And there comes a point where the very values we are defending against terrorism are in danger of being undermined by the measures we are forced to take. Jesus also said, 'Do not fear those who kill the body . . . rather fear him who can destroy both soul and body' (Matthew 10.28). The government says it will have to suspend or curtail these civil liberties and human rights until the war on terrorism is won, but as we know, this is not a war with any identifiable goal, a war we can win by physically obliterating the enemy. As the Egyptian President pointed out, every terrorist killed breeds a hundred more. It was reported in the US that of 700 people detained under terrorist legislation, only ten had actually been charged and brought before the courts – which means that 690 citizens, their families and friends, have good cause to feel aggrieved at their treatment and are hardly likely to be well disposed to their government and society. This is the soil in which the seeds of subversion can easily be planted.

This is a war of ideas and of values in which the terrorist has only one power – admittedly, it is a fearsome one, to kill and destroy at random. Beyond that, any damage terrorism achieves is likely to be done by us in reaction to it. One way we can preserve our soul intact in a free society is by seeing that strict justice is done even to those who are sworn to destroy us.

This whole murky area between what is acceptable interrogation and what is torture has been blurred even more by a ruling of the Court of Appeal in 2004 that under certain conditions evidence obtained by outright torture can be used against these detainees, provided that the torture is done by someone else, not by British authorities. One can almost hear the sound of splashing water as Pontius Pilate washes his hands.

There is a rhetorical question politicians love to ask: what sort of a signal will this send out? Well, if I were an interrogator operating well out of the public gaze and eager to get compelling evidence against suspected terrorists, on the basis of the Court of Appeal's ruling I would hardly go out and buy a pair of kid gloves. The terrorism laws which Parliament has approved only require that there be reasonable grounds to suspect that detainees have links with terrorism – this is much lower than the standard of proof needed to convict them in a criminal court. Can anyone know beyond a shadow of a doubt that every one of these people is guilty? After all, in a quite different context, the Court of Appeal has recently been granting posthumous pardons to convicted murderers who were hanged and then turned out to be innocent.

It would be churlish not to acknowledge what is being done on our behalf by the government and security services to protect Britain against terrorism, and silly to expect this battle against terrorism to be fought according to the Queensbury Rules, but if using evidence obtained by torture is acceptable, what is ruled out? This after all is one of the reasons given for the invasion of Iraq in the first place – that Saddam Hussein was a tyrant who tortured his victims. With what integrity can we condemn regimes around the world that use imprisonment without trial and torture if we are complicit in such abominable practices ourselves?

Are we like Faustus, selling our soul to the Devil? To paraphrase Jesus: how can the methods of Satan drive out Satan?

Tiptoeing through the Minefield

There can be no doubt about the sincerity and fervour of President Bush's devotion to Jesus Christ. In his book *A Charge to Keep* he describes his decision to commit his heart to Jesus Christ. He traces this to a discussion he had as he walked along a beach in Maine with Dr Billy Graham. He was, he said, 'humbled to learn that God had sent his Son to die for a sinner like me'. He then joined a Bible class. Later, he describes how he and his wife went and 'stood atop the hill where Jesus delivered the Sermon on the Mount. It was an overwhelming feeling to stand in the spot where the most famous speech in the history of the world was delivered, the spot where Jesus outlined the character and conduct of a believer and gave his disciples and the world the beatitudes, the Golden Rule and the Lord's Prayer.' He concludes that faith had changed his life and enabled him 'to build on a foundation that will not shift'.[1]

That is an account of the classical evangelical experience and as such should be respected. But in the light of what we know about the White House Bible group's attitude to the Scriptures, it is fair to ask just how deeply they have delved into the historical context

---

1 George W. Bush, *A Charge to Keep*, William Morrow & Co., 1999, quoted in Peter Singer, *The President of Good and Evil*, Granta, 2004.

of the life and ministry of Jesus of Nazareth. Are they aware, for instance, that the only hard fact about his life corroborated by non-Christian historians of the time is that he was executed as a Jewish nationalist for stirring up rebellion against the Roman government of Judea? The Gospels were written by men with an axe to grind. They were anxious to prove false the charge that Jesus was a freedom fighter against Rome. But their attempts to establish him as the innocent dupe of crafty Jewish ecclesiastical foxes ring so hollow it is not easy to imagine they believed it themselves.

The Jesus of the Gospels seems to sail through the upper air, serenely isolated from the politics of his day, exchanging repartee about worship, theology and personal morality. In fact, he lived at the heart of a battleground across which a running war was fought for much of his lifetime. Is it not odd that according to the Gospels he was asked to pronounce on such rarefied issues as the heavenly marital state of a woman with a number of earthly husbands, but no one asked him the more obvious and practical question of whether the Zealots were justified in creating havoc by their violent attacks on the Romans?

Granted, by the time the Gospels were written, the Jewish revolt against Rome had ended, or in the case of Mark, was about to end. And the Gospels were not concerned with by-gone Jewish politics but with presenting Jesus as the saviour of the world. We know what Jesus meant for the time the Gospels were written, but what did he mean for his own time? Did he really tiptoe through a minefield, ignoring the noise and explosions as he pondered the lilies of the field? If Jesus was oblivious of all the violence around him, or regarded it as unimportant, then our efforts to make him relevant to the life of our time are futile because he was irrelevant to the life of *his* time. And to make matters worse, he made ambiguous or provocative statements that invited bloody retaliation upon his followers, all the while protesting he was being misunderstood.

Consider, for example, the testimony of Flavius Josephus, a Jew and a Pharisee who went over to the Roman side and was a sort of adviser to Titus, son of the Roman Emperor. In his later days he became a Roman citizen and devoted his time to writing. About the time Luke was compiling his Gospel, Josephus published an account of the Jewish wars against the Romans, and a decade later his history of the Jews from the Creation to the end of the Jewish War – *The Antiquities of the Jews.* He was an eyewitness of much of the Jewish struggle for freedom, and though he made no secret of his Roman sympathies, he strikes the reader as neither a coward nor a sycophant. He obviously thought Jewish resistance to Rome was wasteful of life and property.

The moral of his story of the Jews during Jesus' lifetime was a simple one. Disaster overtook the Jewish nation at the fall of Jerusalem in 70 CE because of the disruptive activities of the Zealots, Jewish freedom fighters. He concedes that the Zealots 'had an invincible love of liberty for they held God to be their only Lord and Master' – a sentiment Jesus must have echoed from the bottom of his heart. The opening round of their long struggle coincided with the setting of Luke's account of the Nativity – the decree from Caesar Augustus that a census of the Jewish people should be taken for tax purposes. In Luke's Gospel this movement of the people to their cities of origin explains why Jesus was born in Bethlehem. 'All went to their own towns to be registered,' says Luke (2.3). Not all of them. Many Jews refused to submit to the census and a bloody struggle against the Romans took place, led by Judas Gamala.

So behind the Nativity scene with its adoring shepherds and browsing sheep there passes unnoticed in the Gospels a bloody battle that marked the Zealots' hopeless struggle for freedom. From this time on, wrote Josephus, 'The whole nation grew mad with distemper,' adding that there were no less than 10,000 violent disorders in Judea.

Galilee, though not directly under Roman rule, was the most

virulent hot-bed of Zealot activity. Josephus comments, 'Their inhabitants were inured to warfare from infancy.' The hymn writer rhapsodizes, 'O Sabbath rest by Galilee, O calm of hills above.' In fact, Galilee was electric with defiance, the scene of plotting and strife, her 'calm hills' the refuge of guerrilla fighters. Jesus grew to adulthood in an atmosphere vibrant with militancy and must have been educated on the legends of the Galilean freedom fighters as well as the Jewish Law.

The cross was a badge of Zealot defiance long before it became a Christian symbol. Hundreds of freedom fighters died by crucifixion. When Jesus warned that those who followed him must be prepared to take up their crosses, the reference must have been unmistakable, not just to spiritual self-denial but also to harsh physical suffering.

It is beyond belief that Jesus was unaffected by this Zealot tradition which held fanatically to the right to be free and the liberty to worship the only true God. Among the Jewish people there were four main attitudes to Rome, represented by the Sadducees who were open collaborators, the Pharisees who hated the Romans but were awaiting supernatural vindication by the arrival of the Messiah, the Herodians, supporters of the puppet-king of Galilee, and the Zealots who were prepared to fight and die for freedom. According to the Gospels, Jesus condemned the Sadducees, Pharisees and Herodians on a number of occasions, sometimes collectively, at other times separately. Nowhere in the Gospels is there any reference to Jesus condemning the Zealots who were setting the nation alight. It is a matter of record that he chose at least one Zealot to be a member of his inner circle, named Simon the Canaanite by Mark (3.18), but identified openly as Simon the Zealot by Luke (6.15), who was writing after the dust had settled and the Zealot rebellion had passed into history.

Take the crux of the issue, the trial of Jesus for sedition. Mark is almost agonized to show that Jesus was a political innocent who at no time got involved in subversive actions against the Romans; it was the Jewish authorities who rigged the whole thing to trick the Roman authorities into doing their dirty work for them. Pontius Pilate was the scapegoat, a decent but weak character, personally convinced of Jesus' innocence but trapped into executing him when the ploy of offering to release a prisoner backfired.

The Pilate of the Gospels is portrayed as a hand-wringing vacillator in whose character decency and cowardice are at war. This is not how his contemporaries saw him. According to Philo, he was a nasty piece of work with vast experience of waging war against Jewish freedom fighters and matching wits against the Temple authorities. He would not be easily tricked by the high priests. He had enough on his plate without becoming embroiled in a domestic Jewish squabble, so if Jesus was the political innocent Mark claims, Pilate was tough enough to send the Jewish authorities packing. But if he tried and condemned Jesus, then he thought either the charge of sedition was true or at least that Jesus was a politically dangerous character, who was better got out of the way.

Then there is the curious episode of Barabbas. To show that Pilate wanted to give Jesus a fair chance of escaping death, Mark has him invoking a custom of dubious historicity whereby a prisoner was released at Passover time as an act of clemency. Barabbas was in gaol as a murderous freedom fighter. Mark says that Pilate hoped the people would choose to free Jesus rather than Barabbas. But Pilate would have been a raving madman to give such a dangerous character an even chance of freedom. Colonial overlords don't go around releasing deadly opponents at the height of a bloody freedom struggle in deference to the custom of a religion they don't believe in.

And if Jesus was as remote from the freedom struggle as Mark claims, it would be a fantastic misjudgement on Pilate's part to assume that a rebellious populace would ask for his release rather than that of a rabid nationalist. This would be like the Israelis offering a crowd of militant Palestinians a choice between freeing a leader of Hamas or the Archbishop of Jerusalem. No disrespect to the learned and holy cleric, but he would be the first to agree he must come second in a popularity poll against the leader of a popular uprising. It is not easy to credit Mark's explanation that Pilate *assumed* that if he gave the people a choice between Barabbas and Jesus they would choose Jesus.

In early Christian propaganda, a tremendous amount hung on the fact that Jesus was innocent of sedition. The opening verse of Mark's Gospel, 'The beginning of the good news of Jesus Christ, *the Son of God*', indicates that Jesus had by then come to be regarded as divine, and Paul, whose thought dominated the Church (except in Jerusalem), had interpreted Christ's death as the key to a scheme of universal salvation whose nub was that the utterly innocent one had died sacrificially for the guilty. So there was considerable theological pressure on the writers of the Gospels to show that Jesus had been unjustly condemned and executed. Of course, even if he had been legally condemned, this would not necessarily strike a mortal blow against the doctrine of his atoning work, but it does blur the neat edges of the salvation scheme by introducing all kinds of political issues that many Christians including President Bush would find very unsettling.

It is arguable that Pilate was right to put Jesus to death for sedition. Luke, writing when the Jewish War had passed into history, details the charges against Jesus in a way that makes his trial more explicable – stirring up the people, refusing to pay tribute and claiming political messiahship. Luke obviously thought these charges fantastic, but had Pilate the slightest suspicion about Jesus' involvement in such acts he would have executed him out of hand. And this is precisely what he did.

Because Mark was writing from Rome at the time the Jewish War was reaching its bloody climax, he had some tough explaining to do, particularly about the Roman execution of Jesus for sedition. The lives of the Christian community in Rome could well have depended on his skill in showing that the execution of

Jesus was a tragic mistake. He lays the blame on the Jewish authorities who plot Jesus' downfall, and explains how Pilate is by mischance persuaded to have him killed. The party line is that Jesus was never disloyal to Rome; it was the Jews who were to blame for betraying him – so were sown the early seeds of anti-Semitism that have caused the Jews endless suffering ever since.

So an explanation of Jesus' death designed to meet the needs of Roman Christians in 71 CE became the orthodox view of the Church and was reinforced by the demands of orthodoxy – Jesus was the incarnate Son of God who, being sinless, died to save the world. And because this was his divine mission, he kept himself remote from the domestic political issues of the day.

There is no evidence that Jesus was involved in the freedom struggle of the Zealots, though some of his actions such as the triumphal entry into Jerusalem were highly ambiguous, given the messianic expectations of the Jewish people. We make much of the point that Jesus' own understanding of messiahship and that of the crowds thronging the festival were widely divergent. But the point at issue is not what Jesus thought he was doing, but whether the crowds had any justification for thinking he was doing something different.

However exalted the idea of messiahship set out in the Old Testament at its most profound, for over a century the Jewish people had been schooled to expect a Messiah whose role had strongly political aspects. He was a liberator who would drive out the Roman invader and restore Israel's lost glory. Jesus must have known the political connotations placed by ordinary Jews on the role of the Messiah, yet he chose to ride into Jerusalem in a solemn journey loaded with biblical symbolism, solemnly acting out the messianic role at a time when the popular mood was at its most militant. Could the ordinary man and woman in the street be expected to detect the Suffering Servant through the garb of a political liberator? Would Jesus have raised false hopes by sparking off a demonstration that was bound to misfire and might lead, through patriotic fervour, to a bloody confrontation with the Roman forces?

Perhaps the mission of Jesus was not as straightforwardly spiritual as it was portrayed by the early Church; they may have chosen to suppress any complexities because that did not jell with the image they were at pains to portray – the image of the innocent Lamb led to the slaughter. We shall never know. There was no doubt about Jesus' prime motivation, to proclaim and embody God's kingly rule, but that must have touched the political life of the nation at some points, especially in a time of ferment and rebellion.

I think we need to look closely at what the Gospels do and do not say before endorsing Jesus as the divine standard bearer of the West's imperial mission to the rest of the world, especially if he himself was not neutral in an ancient struggle against an imperial power.

Render unto Caesar

One incident seems to challenge the notion that Jesus had some sympathy with the Zealots who were fighting for freedom against the Roman invaders. According to Mark (12.13), the Pharisees and Herodians try to trap Jesus into declaring his position on the most explosive issue of the day – 'Is it right to pay tribute to Caesar?' According to Josephus, the position of the Zealots was absolute; they would not even touch a coin with Caesar's superscription on it, let alone put a cent into Rome's coffers. The trap was simple. If Jesus said it was right for the Jews to pay tribute he would lose his popular following; if, on the other hand, he said it was wrong, he had given clear evidence of sedition. His answer, 'Give to Caesar what is Caesar's, and to God what is God's,' is taken by Mark to show that he is not guilty of sedition; the Jews could pay tribute to Rome without being disloyal to God.

The playwright David Hare who, though an agnostic, has made a close study of the teaching of Jesus for dramatic purposes wrote:

> Jesus Christ was prone to making comments which seem to support an almost infinite variety of exegesis. A remark like 'Render unto Caesar the things that are Caesar's and unto God the things that are God's' could almost have been produced by computer scientists working at the cutting edge of linguistic theory to formulate the single human sentence responsive to the greatest imaginable number of readings.[1]

---

1 Hare, *Obedience, Struggle and Revolt*, p. 235.

Yet that epigram has become the corner-stone of a theological doctrine of the state which grants it legitimate sovereignty in its own sphere. Lord Acton wrote, 'These words give the state, under the protection of conscience, a sacredness it had never enjoyed and bounds it had never acknowledged.'

One has only to ask: what, in the eyes of a devout Jew, belonged to Caesar in the Holy Land? The answer is – nothing. The Romans had invaded the land of a free people, they ruled by no other sanction than force and extracted tribute as a form of robbery. Throughout their long history, the Jews had never wavered in their belief that everything that touched their lives, their land, the people and its wealth belonged to God. If God had his due, Caesar would get nothing.

If Mark is reporting a genuine saying of Jesus, the form of his answer might seem ambiguous, but its meaning, given the mood of the people, was clearly seditious. It is as though members of the Underground in occupied Europe asked a patriot whose judgement they respected whether they ought to help the Nazis ransack their country of its treasures, and had received the reply, 'Give the Nazis what is coming to them!' An enemy, unfamiliar with the idiom, might find the answer innocent but the questioners would recognize fighting talk when they heard it.

Tribute was not an academic issue. The lives and liberty of Jews depended upon their attitude to it. It would be criminally irresponsible of Jesus to confuse the people in order to make a nice debating point against the Pharisees and Herodians. He would weigh his words with great care and take full responsibility for the advice he gave.

Two other details strengthen this view, one trivial, the other, important. In order to make his point, Jesus has to send someone away to fetch a coin. He was carrying no money. It might have been sheer accident, but it is just possible that he shared the Zealot conviction that it was disloyal to God to touch or handle coinage issued by the Romans and bearing a heathen superscription.

The more important point is that the people were obviously satisfied with his answer, and gave him a rousing welcome when he entered Jerusalem. They may have misunderstood the nature of his messiahship but never for a second would they countenance a collaborator with Rome as God's chosen leader. Therefore, they must have interpreted the answer of Jesus to the Pharisees and Herodians as a resounding 'No!'

If Jesus would have been regarded by the Romans as guilty of sedition against the state, then President Bush's Bible class has some disturbing words and actions to confront.

The Use and Abuse of the Bible

There has never been a President in the White House so outspoken about his Christian faith, nor one who spelt out so explicitly the religious principles on which his actions are based, as George W. Bush. The words of Jesus are openly invoked when public policies are discussed, because as he has said, a President 'should speak for the power of faith'. He believes in 'a divine plan that supersedes all human plans'. And it is not just pious rhetoric. When in April 2004 the crew of a US Navy surveillance plane was detained in China after a mid-air collision, the President's first concern was whether he could get Bibles to them.

Many of the President's key cabinet members are conservative Christians and it is reported that as a result of a deliberate recruiting campaign, a substantial proportion of the junior staff at the White House have been drawn from Christian universities and colleges Evangelical in ethos and tradition. One Senator from the opposition party commented rather biliously, 'One has only to look at Iran or Afghanistan in the days under Taliban control to see what the US would look like saddled with a government run by religious fundamentalists.'

His critics claim that the President is so overtly religious that he is in danger of breaching the American Constitution which carefully separates the powers of Church and state, as for instance when he gave funds from the Federal Government to support the social work of religious organizations. In fairness it should be noted that he has not been sectarian in doling out the cash. As he said before signing the order, 'If a charity is helping the needy, it should not matter if there is a rabbi on the board or a cross or a crescent on the wall, or a religious commitment in the charter. The days of discriminating against religious groups just because they are religious are coming to an end.'

Such views have made him the target of religious groups to his right who regard him as a dangerous liberal. President Bush is far from being a fundamentalist; too far, according to these critics. As one would expect in a big country which embraces wide extremes of opinion and conviction, there are groups in the United States on the wilder shores of religious fervour who dismiss the President as barely Christian at all. They believe his attitude to the word of God is too permissive; he should be applying it literally dot and comma rather than in vague generalities. And his cautious attempts since the 11 September atrocity to plead for tolerance towards Arab-Americans were contemptuously dismissed as encouraging the worship of a false god, Allah.

While there are Christians in the United States as well as in Britain who worry about the way President Bush uses the Bible as an instrument of policy, it is a matter of simple justice to him to take account of some of the grotesque misinterpretations of Scripture on public record which purport to prove that he is virtually the Anti-Christ.

Some of his Christian accusers specialize in numerology and base their attack on Revelation 13.18 which runs: 'Calculate the number of the beast, for it is the number of a person. Its number is six hundred and sixty-six.' By assigning each of the 26 letters of the alphabet a number and then applying them to the name 'George Walker Bush' these Bible scholars arrive at the number 6. Then he was born on 6 July 1946, so add up all the digits in his date of birth and you get 3 plus 3, the second 6. Then take the date on which he was elected to his first public office, the governorship of Texas, and by the same process you arrive at the third 6. Alternatively, there is another 6 in reserve, derived from the date he was elected President. Behold the result is 666, the number of the beast. This analysis was published in a journal with a wide circulation among biblical literalists.

On the misuse of the Bible, David Hare comments:

> The Bible is often treated like some massive, incoherent natural resource, a kind of philosophical building skip full of old planks and plumbing, waiting to be looted for purely private purposes by any old mad woman with a handbag who happens to come along. No wonder it is a book which has traditionally provided so much inspiration to raving loonies in the street.[1]

We may scorn the bizarre nonsense of the numerologists, but there are God-fearing, Bible-believing Christians in significant numbers in the United States who buy and read the publications which contain this sort of stuff. And they are also voters on whom the President and his advisers must keep a wary eye. It wouldn't be surprising if in the secret watches of the night George Bush envies some of his predecessors who were agnostics or humanists, about whom the religious constituency would have to make up its mind on more pragmatic grounds. By definition, only believers can blaspheme. If you don't believe in God, it is no more blasphemous to insult him than to mock Father Christmas; you may cause great offence, but that is not blasphemy. So Presidents who make no claim to religious belief may be destined for hell but at least they will be spared the execration called down on liberal Christian heads of state by the fundamentalists.

There are immense dangers in using the Bible as a textbook of public policy, and not simply because you have moved on to the ground of religious fanatics whose obsession and delight is slugging it out text by text, word by word. If you brush aside critical scholarship and aren't too bothered about the context from

---

1 Hare, *Obedience, Struggle and Revolt*, p. 235.

which you wrench a Bible verse, you can use it to prove *anything*. I came across a verse the other day which some preacher with a strong stomach might choose as his text for a sermon at a service celebrating multi-religious co-operation: 'If . . . your most intimate friend [says], "Let us go and worship other gods" . . . you must not yield to or heed any such [person]. Show them no pity or compassion and do not shield them. But you shall surely kill them. . . . Stone them to death for trying to turn you away from the Lord your God' (Deuteronomy 13.6–10).

Or the fundamentalists must wrestle with this verse from the prophet Ezekiel in which God determines to punish his people by deliberately giving them laws which would lead them into evil: 'Moreover, I gave them statutes that were not good and ordinances by which they could not live . . . that they might know that I am the Lord' (Ezekiel 20.25–6).

This question of the use and abuse of the Bible is critical at a time when society seems to be without any moral compass. President Bush has staked his credibility on the Bible as a guide to specific social issues. But take just one, highlighted by American homosexuals fighting for same-sex marriage. They trawled through the Bible to get one authoritative view about marriage and produced this list: widows should refrain from sexual intimacy for the rest of their lives (1 Timothy 5.5–15); marriage between people of different faiths is absolutely banned (Deuteronomy 7.3); a man should not marry a woman who is unwilling to obey his every whim (Ephesians 5.22; Titus 2.3); a minister may only marry a virgin (Leviticus 21.13), and a rapist must marry his victim (Deuteronomy 22.28). And so it goes on.

The truth, unpalatable to some Christians, is that society has moved on in the past 2,000 years. The Bible is not God's last word. He did not relapse into unfathomable silence when the last full-stop was added to the sacred manuscript. Though the slogan, 'The Unchanging Faith in a Changing World' is a favourite evangelical conference theme, the Christian faith has never been fixed, set in stone, immovable. It has always had to adapt itself to the thought forms of the culture in which it is set. Thus, Christianity converted the Greco-Roman world but in the process its own theology was transformed from that of a sub-sect of Judaism into a sophisticated set of ideas expressed in the concepts of Greek philosophy. And the evidence of that accommodation is to be found in later books of the Bible.

In medieval times, the Bible, Christian doctrine and liturgy were all interpreted in the light of tenth-century ideas about the universe and human nature. Far from there being an unchanging faith and doctrinal consistency between medieval Christianity and our own, much of what was thought orthodox in the tenth century would be virtually unintelligible and unbelievable today.

And for the past three centuries, the Church has had to modify its thinking to come to terms with the evolving laws of modern science. The ways in which Christians regard divine providence, miracles, natural law, disease or the location of heaven and hell have been drastically modified, sometimes in the teeth of the literal words of Scripture. Even now, the Christian doctrine of creation is being rethought as environmental threats of almost apocalyptic proportions impinge on our society's consciousness. All these scientific insights have not merely forced marginal adjustments to theology, they have revolutionized the Christian understanding of the nature of God.

The heading of this chapter is actually the title of an important book about biblical criticism by Dr Dennis Nineham.[2] In it he quotes Professor Leonard Hodgson who said that the Bible should always be approached with one question in mind: 'What must the truth be now if people who thought as they did put it like that?' This is the nearest we can get to relating what the Bible says to the contemporary world.

I do not believe that we can derive from the Bible any distinctive

---

2 Dennis Nineham, *The Use and Abuse of the Bible*, Macmillan, 1976.

Christian political policies, but I do believe there is a distinctive Christian imperative to do our duty in the political realm, trusting in the Spirit of God to guide us into the truth.

Crucified or Crusading Mind?

It has been reported that one of President Bush's favourite texts is taken from Paul's Letter to the Philippians: 'Let the same mind be in you that was in Christ Jesus' (2.5). There is a minor irony in the fact that Philippians was written from prison; had Paul been incarcerated in Abu Graib, the gaol run by the Americans in Iraq, he would have been denied anything to write with. Philippians was also addressed to the first congregation Paul established on European soil. President Bush is no lover of Europe which he feels, with the exception of one or two countries, failed to support him in the United Nations or on the ground in Iraq.

Those are just debating points. There can be no more important task for the Christian than to discern the mind of Christ. The Japanese theologian Kosuke Koyama has described it as a crucified rather than a crusading mind. He has inherited the tradition of an Eastern people who have been on the receiving end of the European missionary enterprise. The Western mind is an aggressive, thrusting, problem-solving mind. Cocksureness, intellectual and spiritual imperialism, the compulsion to overwhelm those cultures that were resistant to the gospel – these are the components of one of the less admirable, though persistent, strands in Christian history.

The crusading mind needs enemies it can engage and subdue. All my life, people have been warning of some great external threat to our society. During the cold war it was Soviet Communism, then when I went to Africa, white settlers told me that African nationalism would bring civilization crashing and usher in a new age of barbarism. Now according to a book that has reached the best-seller list in the United States, we are in for a re-run of the Crusades. Islam is the enemy.

The crusading mind systematizes. It can scoop up and label countless unique personalities, reducing them to an abstraction – Communism, Islam, Christianity: systems of ideas we can sum up neatly in our minds and then pronounce good or evil. It is easy to make an enemy of an abstraction on to which we can project our fears. It is a different matter when we are confronted not by Communism but by a Communist, not by Islam but a Muslim. There is much more to a living person than the label he or she wears. This is the point Jesus was making when he said that human beings are more than the Sabbath and that he was greater than the Temple. He meant that human beings are more important, more mysterious, than the systems, the 'ologies' and 'isms' that seek to contain them. This the crusading mind finds it hard to accept.

The crucified mind by contrast is diffident, almost timid in its judgements about people, always conscious of the mystery of the other as a personality with its own rights, perceptions of the truth and hidden agonies. It is the openness and vulnerability of the crucified mind that makes it sensitive to the needs of others, a quality well demonstrated by Jesus who when being pressed on all sides by a crowd asks, 'Who touched me?' the instant a woman in pain grasped the hem of his robe.

In his monumental *Study of History*, Arnold Toynbee makes great play of what he terms the Aeschylean Clue to the understanding of human development – a moral he derives from the works of the Greek tragedian: all learning comes through suffering. This explains the evolution of the crucified mind which accepts gratefully all the experiences of life, pain and pleasure, bane and blessing, and turns them to good account, regretting nothing except what is futile and repenting only what is sinful.

This is surely what the author of the Letter to the Hebrews meant when he wrote that Jesus 'learned obedience through what he suffered' (5.8). Life's blows did not cow him, but certainly filled him with 'godly fear', to use the Letter's phrase. The crucified mind is fine-tuned by suffering whereas the crusading mind is hardened against it and is impoverished because it rejects what Isaiah describes so exquisitely as 'the treasures of darkness' (Isaiah 45.3).

Note the variety of ways in which Jesus deals with people in the Gospels. Sometimes he is content to meet their immediate need. Bartimaeus receives his sight, the leper is cleansed, the epileptic boy is healed, Jairus' daughter is raised from the dead. Yet so far as we know, he made no request or demand that they should become his disciples. At other times, his demand is radical – 'Leave your nets!' or 'Sell all that you have and give to the poor!' Why the difference? The crusading mind would be unequivocal in its claims; all have heard, all who ask have received, therefore all must obey. The crucified mind has a much finer appreciation of human strengths and weaknesses. It senses who will carry the cross to the end or collapse under its weight; who will bury God's treasure in a field or use it fruitfully; who among those who cry Lord! Lord! will act to the limit of their confession. Why? Not because it is a superior or supernatural mind but because it had registered the adulation of the crowd, the agony in the garden, the pain of betrayal, the full power of redemption and the final vindication through obedience unto death.

For much of the time it seems to be the crusading mind of the West which is directing the war in Iraq. It is brilliant at deploying the technology, superb at organizing personnel and material and at co-ordinating a complex battle plan. But innocent people die, towns are devastated and one of the world's most ancient cultures is disrupted. The stated aim of the coalition forces is 'to win the hearts and minds of the Iraqi people'. To have a ghost of a chance of success they will have to bring to the encounter not the proud assertiveness of the crusading mind but the humility and sensitivity of the crucified mind. That's the mind you need, says Paul.

Flawed Intelligence

There have now been no less than five enquiries of one sort or another into the failure of British intelligence to get to the truth of the claims, which proved to be unfounded, about Saddam Hussein's access to weapons of mass destruction. The latest, headed by Lord Butler, concluded that such intelligence as there was left the headquarters of MI6 qualified by caveats and larded with doubts, but somehow by the time it got into the hands of the politicians, all hesitations were gone, probabilities had become imperatives: Saddam had weapons capable of being deployed against British targets in 45 minutes.

Many questions have been raised and suspicions voiced in the aftermath of these reports, but one obvious question has never been asked. Why does a liberal democracy need intelligence at all, with or without caveats? That is a question which takes us beyond politics and security into the realms of theology.

Gathering intelligence is polite-speak for the stealing of secrets that belong to others, for our own protection. It seems to be a tragic necessity in a corrupted world where nothing is what it seems, where nations cannot trust one another, where every country is thought to have a secret agenda, where national pride and large egos clash. And it is not just our enemies we mistrust. It was revealed that the office of the Secretary General of the United Nations had been bugged.

It is doubly tragic that the fallen human nature which requires that we use intelligence to defend ourselves also pollutes the intelligence process itself, so it comes to depend upon the lowest of motives, bribery, treachery, betrayal and double-dealing. Of course, there is nobility too. We thankfully acknowledge the men and women whose bravery and sacrifice we the public will never hear about. Nevertheless, the most telling comment about the prevailing morality of that secret world was made by an ex-head of the Central Intelligence Agency after the 9/11 bombings. He said it was almost impossible for the CIA to penetrate Al Qa'eda cells because they were made up of fanatical religious believers in Islam and therefore they were hard to bribe and corrupt.

Journalists often complain that there is too much secrecy about, and it makes life hard for them as they try to give a truthful and complete account of what is going on. They quote what has become a cliché of the media age – 'The public has a right to know.' What does that mean? What kind of a 'right' is it that the public has? Given the almost limitless amount of knowledge in the world, the public's right to it is as unenforceable as a claim to own property on Mars.

The public undoubtedly has the right to know about anything that affects the common welfare. Since the government is the chief repository of such information and has more power to affect people's lives than any other institution, it is right that the public should know what the government is up to. And they have this right because it is *their* knowledge; the government is simply the community acting politically. Even when the government holds back some information on the grounds of national security, it may still be required to demonstrate to someone acting on behalf of the community, a security commission or a High Court judge, that the people's welfare is not threatened by their ignorance. Otherwise, citizens have no way of knowing whether such secrecy is justified or not, because by definition not only the content of a secret but its very existence is hidden from them. That combination of great power and utter secrecy which governments possess is a very dangerous thing; it offers the constant temptation to tyranny.

Two specific restraints on the public's right to know are secrecy and privacy. We tend to use the terms interchangeably though they are different things. The core of secrecy is intentional concealment; that of privacy is deliberate exclusion. Secrecy, as its Latin root suggests, is the setting aside from the common store of knowledge certain information, possession of which constitutes power and whose loss makes one vulnerable. Privacy on the other hand is a territorial right. It is the claim to a personal domain from which the public is excluded. What is private is not necessarily secret. A private garden may be quite visible from the road; the public just won't be allowed in. A personal diary might be private but not secret. It lies there on a table in the confidence that no unauthorized person will read it. A private diary would also become secret if it were written in code or hidden away somewhere.

Privacy, unlike secrecy, is not bound up with what one possesses but with who one is. It safeguards personal identity, the distinction between I and Not-I. Every human being is entitled to some inviolate inner sanctum to which no one else has access except by invitation.

It could be argued that ours is a society in which there is too much secrecy and not enough privacy, largely thanks to the tabloid press, which has distorted the idea of the public's right to know to the point where basic decencies are flouted by a prurient intrusiveness. The handling of privacy is a critical issue in the media age. It requires discretion, not in the conventional meaning of good manners but in the stronger sense of the intuitive ability to navigate between everybody's private and shared worlds and to know what properly belongs to each. Even in an open society, there is something to protect – the sacred, the intimate, the fragile, the dangerous and the forbidden. Careless disclosure in these areas produces not just scandal but shame.

It is necessary to defend the sacred right of privacy even in the act of challenging the necessity of so much secrecy in the modern government's dealings. The historian Lord Acton wrote: 'Everything secret degenerates. Nothing is safe that cannot bear public scrutiny and discussion.' He could have been echoing Jesus who knew what was in the human heart and would have nothing to do with secret strategies. Again and again, he used the metaphors of light and darkness. He said it is of the nature of goodness even when done by stealth to thrust upwards towards the light, whereas evil prefers the safety of darkness where it can flourish in obscurity. He said that there is nothing hidden that will not be revealed, and that his followers should be the children of light, everything they do open to public scrutiny as though to the eyes of God.

Jesus' vision might be dismissed as hopelessly idealistic, but it raises a troubling question which ties in with the discussion of intelligence in the Butler Report. In the war against terror, to what extent can a free society where traditionally most things are done in the light pursue the strategies of darkness without creating murky places in which more terrorists will breed than can be rooted out?

Part Three – 24/7

'The Least Bad Form of Government'

At his second inauguration speech in 2004, President George W. Bush said that he has two foreign policy aims: to destroy international terrorism and to spread democracy to those parts of the world, especially the Middle East, that do not enjoy it. And because the President is a devout, Bible-reading Christian, he has declared that democracy is the God-ordained form of government, of which the United States is the supreme example and which it has a sacred duty to spread to the rest of the world.

President Bush is not alone in claiming that democracy is *the* Christian form of government. In the last century, Christians who believed in what was called the social gospel offered descriptions of an earthly kingdom of God which was virtually indistinguishable from that of a liberal democracy.

In fact, as a matter of history, both Christian and non-Christian thinkers have helped to evolve the theory of liberal democracy. Thus, the chief architects of the constitution of President Bush's own nation, the United States, were the atheist Thomas Jefferson and the Calvinist James Maddison.

What is so special about democracy? Why did Winston Churchill describe it ambiguously as 'the least bad form of government'? In spite of President Bush's ringing endorsement of democracy, the Bible itself does not baptize any particular type of state. As the Old Testament records, the people of Israel in their long journey through history flourished or suffered under many political systems — theocracy (Judges 8), absolute monarchy (1 Samuel 24), anarchy (Judges 21), princeship (Ezekiel 40), slavery (Babylonian captivity), priest-kingship (Maccabees) and imperialism (Rome). The Bible's only interest in any particular form of government seems to have been whether it was the agent of God's righteousness or the rod of his anger.

But there are some aspects of democracy that accord well with Christian principles. For example, democracy is realistic about human nature. Archbishop Reynolds was tragically wrong and thoroughly unbiblical when he declared at the coronation of Edward III, 'The voice of the people is the voice of God!' It is obvious that the voice of the people may be the voice of the Devil as when they cry, 'Give us Barabbas!' or 'Sieg Heil!' Indeed, it is nearer the mark to claim that since no human voice is the voice of God, it is only through the clamour of everyone's voice that some approximation to justice may be achieved. Abraham Lincoln put it in a nutshell: 'No man is good enough to rule another without that other's consent.'

Modern democracy, as the Christian understands it, differs from the classical Greek version in that it takes more account of a human being's *worth* than his or her *wisdom*. Only an elite could vote in Greek democracies. Yet foolish people are not less affected by the policies of government than wise people. Reinhold Niebuhr summarizes the way democracy responds to both human weakness and strength in his famous epigram: 'Man's capacity for justice makes democracy possible, but Man's inclination towards injustice makes democracy essential.' [1]

Democracy, too, differs from totalitarianism because it recognizes that politics is a matter of trial and error. Often a political

---

1 Reinhold Niebuhr, *The Children of Light and the Children of Darkness*, Nisbet, 1945, p. vi.

policy can't be pronounced right or wrong in principle; it is only in the light of its consequences that the morality of a political decision becomes clear. The truth is often complex and more likely to be found in a balance of opposites than in a simple declaration. The historian Lord Acton said, 'When you perceive a truth, look for a balancing truth.' Democracy does make room for this 'balancing truth' through the concept of lawful opposition. So if truth is a matter of trial and error, then democracy through the ballot box can ensure the legal removal of a government whose 'trials' have proved to be 'errors'.

What is sometimes criticized as the inefficiency of democracy may be its ultimate wisdom and safeguard against error, for rarely can any political ideology reach its limit without being modified or changed by the flux of public opinion through the ballot box. This is wisdom because as Niebuhr has said, 'There is an element of truth in every political position which becomes falsehood precisely when it is carried through too consistently.'

Because democracy at its best does not claim to be all-knowing, the Christian within the system is able to criticize and stand against authority in the name of a higher authority. St Peter's declaration in Jerusalem, 'We must obey God rather than any human authority' (Acts 5.29) has a greater chance of being heeded in a democratic system than in any other because democracy can admit, however grudgingly, the possibility of error. Democracy is capable of a humility that the totalitarian state cannot allow because it knows no higher truth than its own ideology.

Then, again, democracy has reconciliation built into it. There are so many competing interests in any society that every single policy adopted by a government will favour some and penalize others. By its very nature, government generates opposition to itself. Once that opposition becomes articulate and organized, the state is in danger of shattering. Democracy lessens that danger through the concept of a Loyal Opposition, by harnessing dissenters constructively in the work of government by allowing them to analyse and comment on programmes as they pass through the legislature.

For this reason, democracy might be described as a peaceful alternative to civil war. Conflicts are hammered out in the legislature instead of on the battlefield. The opposition fights to the very limits of the system for the values it believes are precious, but not beyond those limits, so that it is possible to argue with heat and passion in the chamber and then laugh and chat and share a drink afterwards. And that is not just a social formality; it is saying in effect, when all the conflict is over, what we have in common – our God-given humanity – is more important than our political differences.

By making room for personal reconciliation among those who are political opponents, democracy not only preserves the peace and good order of the community, but testifies to the truth that there is a realm even more important than politics where humanity is being reconciled to God by the power of Christ.

Christianity is the enemy of elitisms, of class, of race, of sex. It insists there is room for all in the father's house; it invites all to receive the grace of the gospel; it declares that Christ can use the gifts and sacrifice of all, without exception, in the service of his kingdom.

So democracy accords well with this New Testament insight about the inclusiveness of the gospel. There are some political systems whose power is vested in a ruling dynasty or a military junta or a master class like Communism or a super race like Fascism. And once that elite is discredited or overthrown, the whole system crashes. Democracy's strength is that it can constantly renew itself because it harnesses the skills and gifts of anybody at any level in society. Its techniques are practised throughout society – debating and voting on policy issues, keeping proper accounts and accurate minutes, electing officers, canvassing people. There are mini-democracies at work in the church, golf club, trade union branch, women's institute, parish council and dozens of community societies. And it is part of the genius of democracy that a man or woman can begin by chairing the local pigeon-fanciers' society and end up presiding at a cabinet meeting in No. 10 Downing Street.

Democracy therefore can provide the sinews of healthy community life through the vitality of a thousand and one small democracies in clubs and societies and organizations which express the distinctive character of a community and, like the threads of a spider's web, bind it together, providing the seedbed of its future leadership.

The great theologian Karl Barth went much further than Winston Churchill in endorsing democracy. He said we would be justified in regarding the democratic conception of the state as 'a justifiable extension of the thought of the New Testament'.

One can therefore understand President Bush's enthusiasm, expressed in a number of speeches, that the aim of the war in Iraq should be to bring democracy to the Muslim world. Reshaping the Middle East is part of America's mission to rewrite history. The problem is that the removal of tyrants in the Middle East may not result in the triumph of Western values in a liberal democracy. As in the case of Algeria, the result is more likely to be a victory for radical Islam. John Gray writes, '[President Bush's policies] augur disaster. For much of the region, the choice is not between tyranny and freedom; it is between theocratic democracy and secular dictatorship.' Thus, if the Coalition forces dislodge a dictator like Saddam Hussein, any democratic system they impose on the people of Iraq is likely to be dominated by the mullahs. In spite of symbols such as ballot boxes and legislative assemblies, any democracy that emerges, because its dominant doctrine will be a version of radical Islam, will still regard America as the Great Satan.

In a speech President Bush has declared that 'America has no empire to extend or utopia to establish. We wish for others only what we wish for ourselves – safety from violence, the rewards of liberty and the hope for a better life.' These are truly admirable sentiments, but it is clear that the President believes these desirable goals can only be achieved by spreading, or even imposing if necessary, liberal democratic values on countries and cultures to whom the system is alien. Influential members of the President's staff talk openly about the need for a *Pax Americana*, global peace guaranteed by military and economic supremacy. Stripped of rhetoric, this means that 5 per cent of the world's population would impose its will on the other 95 per cent. There is nothing very democratic about that.

The greatest contribution Christians can make to the debate about democracy or any other political system is to bring to bear a rigorous realism about the limitations of any form of government, however just and efficient, because it is run and served by sinful human beings. Reinhold Niebuhr wrote:

> The freedom of the spirit must come to terms with the contingencies of nature, the moral ideal must find a proper mechanism for its incarnation and the ideal principle must be sacrificed to guarantee its partial realization.[2]

That is not a comforting conclusion but it is a soundly biblical one which we ignore at our peril as we face up to the challenge of nation building in Iraq or anywhere else.

---

2 Reinhold Niebuhr, *An Interpretation of Christian Ethics*, Harper, 1953, p. 135.

Prisoners of Conscience

There are uncounted numbers of men and women shut away in prisons and camps who have committed no offence other than to have expressed opinions that set them on collision course with the government of their country. Some of them are Christians locked up for practising their faith in regimes that regard Christianity as politically or religiously subversive.

Potentially, all Christians are prisoners of conscience. Their secular allegiance is uncertain, their patriotism is conditional. They have only one absolute loyalty, stated with classical simplicity in Acts 5.29. Peter, when hauled before the authorities in Jerusalem declared: 'We must obey God rather than any human authority'. That is not a rejection of the duties of citizenship, just fair warning that if the crunch comes, the conscience of the Christian is, as Luther put it, 'captive to the Word of God' rather than to the *diktat* of the state.

It would be insufferable arrogance to claim that Christians have cornered the market in moral scruples; that they are the sole embodiment of the conscience of humanity. Prisoners of many faiths and none waste away in gaols throughout the world, often forgotten and unnamed. But the Christian faith offers important insights on this issue of human rights; it sketches out the heroic dimensions of the tragedy of humanity in chains.

How ought Christians to respond to the global problem of the prisoners of conscience?

First, by acknowledging that their concern must be indiscriminate. Many of us tend to suffer from what the psychologists call tunnel vision and so elevate our personal prejudices to the status of absolute principles. I come from socialist stock and therefore I found the excesses of Communism, though regrettable, less abhorrent than those of Fascism. I had some association with the black freedom movement in the part of Africa in which I served as a missionary, so I called down the wrath of God on white racism south of the Zambezi but never managed more than a murmur of regret at the black racism north of that river.

Our natural prejudices spill over and infect our language. 'Violence' is what our enemies use against us; 'force' is our response – a distinction without a difference if you happen to be a hapless civilian caught like a nut between the nutcrackers. The Soviet Union used to give those whom we called 'dissidents' but they labelled 'traitors' what is termed 'psychiatric treatment', though those on the receiving end found it indistinguishable from 'torture'. You employ 'terrorists'; we glory in our 'freedom fighters': one nation's 'protective custody' is another's 'detention without trial'.

God has neither favourites nor enemies. He is not the enemy of *my* enemies nor even the enemy of *his* enemies. He will not allow himself to be used, recruited to our colours and borne like the Ark of the Covenant into battle on our side, or any other for that matter. Christian concern must be indiscriminate because God carries no passport. At the level at which his judgement operates, all distinctions between righteous and unrighteous regimes are obscured. All are unceremoniously lumped together and constitute that 'mere drop in the bucket' of which the prophet Isaiah speaks. As he wrote, all nations are shrouded in the 'gross darkness that covers the people' (60.2, AV). This does not absolve us from making responsible moral judgements as citizens, but we must not claim divine sanction for such opinions.

Because they have been created by sinful human beings, all

political systems develop a monstrous egotism and invite idolatry. Hence, the prisoner of conscience, in challenging the state's monopoly of the truth, embodies God's judgement on its pseudo-infallibility. This may be poor consolation to the victim who could be forgiven for railing as much at an uncaring God as against his oppressors, but it lays on us the obligation of cherishing him and her whether we share their convictions or not.

The strongest case for indiscriminate concern is not based on sophisticated theological ideas but on simple evangelical assertions such as the assurance that Christ died for all. If there breathes a person who falls outside the category of the 'all' for whom Christ gave his life, we can safely ignore him. Otherwise our liability is unlimited.

Then, the Christian's compassion must be specific, earthing general principles in particular people with names and faces and stories. This is in line with our understanding of the nature of God who shows a majestic indifference to our national achievements yet notices an injured sparrow fall to the ground and is apparently interested in minutiae such as the number of hairs on our heads.

Christian compassion can never be a generalized sentiment which wreathes the oppressed in a cloud of piety. We can express broad sympathy for millions; but we can only really feel for a few. Yet it is our willingness to suffer with even one as best we can that gives us the right to pronounce on the plight of the rest. Massive concentration on the specific, the effort to discover the name and circumstances of one political prisoner, is our only defence against moral anaesthesia, that numbing of the spirit which steals over us when we try to get our minds round the magnitude of the problem. There are countless thousands of prisoners of conscience. Only God can love them all.

When I worked at the BBC I got to know an actor called David Markham. He told me his story. He was one of a number of public personalities protesting one day outside the Soviet Embassy in London about the imprisonment of dissidents. He was given a placard with the name Vladimir Bukovsky on it. He'd never heard of him, but he became curious about the man whose name he temporarily bore, and decided to find out more. This led him to start a shoe-string campaign to get Bukovsky released. He and his wife wrote hundreds of letters, driven on by the thought of a young Russian sitting through six years of solitary confinement in freezing conditions on a starvation diet. Everything was driven by the simple fact of being able to put a face to a name and a name to an unknown political prisoner. Vladimir Bukovsky was eventually freed. When I asked Mr Markham why he did it, he replied simply, 'For me it was simple: I identified with this man because he represented what was happening.' That is the price of sustained and specific compassion and the possible reward for it.

And the Christian's commitment must be persistent. Even as some prison doors are prised open, others will clang shut. One regime becomes more liberal while another degenerates into tyranny. There will always be a market for barbed wire. That is a doleful conclusion but one in line with the Christian understanding of history which has no room for the assumption that tomorrow will inevitably be better than today. The philosopher John Gray writes, 'History is not an ascending spiral of human advance, or even an inch by inch crawl to a better world. Freedom is recurrently won and lost in an alternation that includes long periods of anarchy and tyranny, and there is no reason to suppose that this cycle will ever end.'

That is what Jesus taught. History is not a success story but a tragedy, which is not to say it is sad but that it forms the arena for a struggle between the forces of spiritual darkness and light. We must do what we can to combat any social evil, even though we know that our very best actions will be twisted in a bent world and let loose a flood of consequences both good and bad. Meanwhile we press on, trying to smash great rocks with our feather dusters, realistic in our expectations but undiscourageable in our persistence. For when every vestige of human achievement or tyranny has been wiped off the face of the earth, it is acts of creative compassion which will be the effectual signs of the presence of the kingdom of heaven.

If We Must Resist

The Iraq War has divided Christians as bitterly as any other part of our society, though most are prepared to give President Bush and the British Prime Minister the benefit of the doubt and accept that though their judgement may have been wrong, their good intentions as God-fearing believers were not in doubt. The two leaders genuinely thought that war was the lesser of two evils, preferable to allowing Saddam Hussein to remain in power and terrorize sections of his population, even if he no longer had any weapons of mass destruction.

But there is talk now of widening the international war on terror. The baleful eye of the US Administration is now cast on Iran and North Korea. Opening up another front in this crusade would undoubtedly be a step too far for most British Christians. For the first time in many years, it may be necessary to bring out and dust off those old tomes in which the Reformers spelt out the theology of Christian resistance. There is a vast literature detailing the story of the costly witness and even martyrdom of individual Christians, but what about tension between the Church as such and the government at a time when it may not welcome what Karl Barth has called the 'wholesomely disturbing presence of the Church'?

We are nowhere near this stage yet. In Britain, this is an exercise as theoretical as one of those civil defence rehearsals for what to do in the event of a nuclear war. But in Zimbabwe, for example, and in other parts of the world, the Church is struggling for its independence and integrity. The question is: if the Church must challenge the state, what are the rules?

Protest. This is the initial stage in the Church's resistance to the state. First, at the infringement of general human rights, whether through colonial adventures abroad or curtailment of civil liberties at home. Here, the essential qualification for sound protest is expert knowledge of the issues involved. The strength of any protest depends upon the Church's ability to analyse an issue and expose a moral defect. We possess no magical divining rod which quivers unerringly at the presence of evil. Pronouncements that are naïve and show ignorance of the technicalities of policy making are rightly brushed aside by the state and lend force to Burke's taunt from his *Reflections on the Revolution in France*: 'Wholly unacquainted with the world in which they are so fond of meddling, and inexperienced in all its affairs, on which they pronounce with such confidence, they [the churches] have nothing of politics but the passions they excite.'

Besides general human rights, there are infringements of gospel freedoms. These constitute the liberty the Church needs to testify to Jesus Christ and spread the gospel. They include: the right to preach and teach according to our beliefs; the right to worship in our own way; the right to call and train ministers; the right to establish links with other churches, and especially with the worldwide Christian fellowship; the right to determine our own membership – all without state interference. These freedoms stem directly out of the word of the gospel, and therefore the Church is on the strongest ground in protesting about any threat to them. They are absolutes, in defence of which we must be prepared to carry our resistance to the limit.

Hard experience teaches a number of lessons about the nature of protest. It needs to be specific. Blanket condemnations have little, if any, value. Karl Barth in his public debate with Emil Brunner on the best way to deal with Communist regimes, an issue which preoccupied European church leaders in the 1950s, warned against protests 'in principle'. 'The Church never thinks, speaks or acts on principle. Rather it judges spiritually and by individual cases. For that reason, it rejects every attempt to systematize political history and its own part in that history. Therefore it preserves the freedom to judge every new event afresh.'

Protest should also be infrequent. We are reminded in the Book of Ecclesiastes that there is 'a time to keep silence, and a time to speak' (3.7). When the Church makes a habit of nagging the state, constantly warning and complaining, the clarity of its prophetic voice is muffled. There should be an almost apocalyptic quality about the tone and infrequency of the Church's challenge. The mere fact that the Church is speaking at all should indicate that government and people face an issue of moral seriousness. And because we can make no claim to infallibility for our judgements, our tone should be one of sympathetic concern, making generous allowance for the heavy load of responsibility the state carries.

Majestic imprecations from a position of non-responsibility are alien to the spirit of Christ. True protest is distinguished from general moralizing because it is uttered from a position of engagement and reveals a willingness to pay the price of an unequivocal stand. A long time ago, Gerald Winstanley, the leader of the Diggers, who knew something of the cost of defying the state, wrote: 'There are but few who act for freedom, and the actors for freedom are oppressed by the talkers and verbal professors of freedom.'

All true protest derives its cutting edge from a willingness to suffer. The spirit of cheap bravado which sometimes characterizes Church protests from a distance against evils it does not itself suffer make little impact. Engaged protest is a currency backed by the lives, liberty and good reputation of those uttering it. Which is why the state would do well to heed it.

Disobedience. This is the next stage in Christian resistance. The spirit which moves a Church or an individual Christian to break the law is much more serious than an act of simple insubordination. If we do disobey the law, we do so in a 'spirit of fear and trembling', not from any failure of courage, but because we know we are challenging the state in its theological identity as an ordinance of God. In one of the second-century Christian writings, the First Epistle of Clement, the author prays that we may be 'obedient to thy almighty and glorious name and to our rulers and governors upon the earth, to whom thou hast given the power of sovereignty through thy excellent and inexpressible might, that we may know the honour given to them by thee, and be subject to them, in nothing resisting thy will'.

That is, literally, an Almighty endorsement of the state's role in the purposes of God. This is why there is an important distinction between the individual Christian's act of disobedience and a call to defiance by the whole Church. For the individual Christian, disobedience is a matter of conscience, and he or she may be proved right or wrong in the end; in any case, the significance of the act is limited. However, when the Church as a body breaks the law it is challenging the state's divine commission; so corporate disobedience must be demonstratively a religious rather than a political act, whose consequences could be far-reaching. Every flouting of the law by a large number of citizens weakens the authority of the state and so may make anarchy more likely.

In the First Letter of Peter, Christians are told: 'Always be ready to make your defence to anyone who demands from you an account of the hope that is in you; yet do it with gentleness and reverence' (3.15–16). Unless the state has shown itself to be utterly demonic, the purpose of acts of disobedience is not to bring a government down but to persuade it to amend its ways. The act should be done 'with gentleness and reverence'. Arrogance, warlike threats and cheap denunciations are totally out of place when confronting officers of the state whom the New Testament describes as 'ministers of God'. John Calvin warns: 'Although the Lord takes vengeance on unbridled domination, let us not therefore suppose that this vengeance is committed to us, to whom no command has been given but to obey and to suffer.'

Because it is the state and not the Church which must bear responsibility for its actions, Christians must never 'chance their arm' on an act of disobedience. Where there is doubt about the wisdom of resistance, the Church should obey the law. The state is entitled to the benefit of the doubt because, as the slang phrase has it, that is where the buck stops.

Suffering. When relations between Church and state deteriorate through constant collision to the point where mutual understanding is impossible, all that is left for the Church to do is to suffer. Even then we are required to do more than meet our fate with the dumb passivity of a captive ox. The most rigid state is not a soulless machine. It is run by people. Its policies are carried out by officials who, unless we have the most pessimistic estimate of human nature, are not totally immune to the influence of love; indeed, the Christian's duty when challenging an authoritarian state is to soften the system with love. One of the heartening themes to emerge from the hell of the Nazi concentration camps was the record of the sheer goodness of religious inmates who, by their loving attitude towards their gaolers, made the lot of some of their fellow prisoners more bearable. Gerhard Leibholz in his memoir of Dietrich Bonhoeffer wrote,

> In prisons and concentration camps, Bonhoeffer greatly inspired by his indomitable courage, his unselfishness and goodness, all those who came into contact with him. He even inspired his guards with respect, some of whom became so attached to him that they smuggled out of prison his papers and poems written there and apologised to him for having to lock his door after the round in the courtyard.[1]

---

1 Gerhard Leibholz, 'Memoir' in Dietrich Bonhoeffer, *The Cost of Discipleship*, SCM Press, 1959, 2001 edition, pp. xiii f.

The gospel was first preached throughout a society in which both the Jewish church and state were opposed to it, yet there are instances where the early Christians were able to soften the system with love. Pilate in the Judgement Hall, the centurion on Golgotha and the gaoler at Philippi were all gripped in the vice of a rigid government system, but each responded to the love of Christ. The command to 'Pray for them that persecute you' is more than an invitation to make a pious gesture; it means we must take pastoral responsibility for our enemies.

When we are helpless to influence the course of events and our pleas are swept aside by a state, we are still not allowed to wash our hands and retire from the fray. At this point we have to bring to bear the Bible's understanding of history, where God often used tyrannical states as instruments of his will. Calvin spells it out in his *Institutes of the Christian Religion*:

> Thus God tamed the pride of Tyre by the Egyptians; the insolence of the Egyptians by the Assyrians; the ferocity of the Assyrians by the Chaldeans; the confidence of Babylon by the Medes and Persians. All these things were not however done in the same way though they were directed by the hand of God, as seemed to him good, and did his work without knowing and had nought but evil in their thoughts.

There is a subterranean theme in history the secular historian knows nothing about, but which the Christian must try to uncover as events transpire. The God who chose to tame and use Cyrus rather than destroy him can bring good out of evil and use the most unlikely of people and institutions for his glory.

Of course, it is no use pretending that even the most profound understanding of history will necessarily make our lot any more comfortable, but it will serve to keep before society the truth that all earthly tyranny is only permitted to persist 'till he come'. We live in the intermediate time between two great events – what God has already done in Jesus Christ the Redeemer and what he intends to do in Jesus Christ the Judge. By our attempts to understand what we cannot change, we shall be delivered from false pride in our ability to create our own destiny, and accept our utter dependence upon the God of history.

The ultimate question is posed when the state challenges the Christian to resistance at any cost. The possibility of 'witnessing unto blood' recurs throughout the New Testament like a drum beat. The Christian is told to show the fearlessness of those who only fear God and to be unafraid of those whose sole power is to destroy the body. The theme of martyrdom is magnificent but it is pointless to pretend that in human terms it always achieves its object. When the modern state brings to bear its great power on those who defy it, it often does so garbed in a righteousness that makes the act of defiance appear treacherous and anti-social. Rarely does the modern martyr enjoy the luxury of a glorious confrontation with a hungry lion. The due process of law and the antiseptic atmosphere of the court room rob martyrdom of much of its drama. Nor need the state exact the ultimate penalty and so allow the Christian to lay down his or her life for Christ's sake. Rather than a great martyrdom, the Christian is likely to suffer a succession of little martyrdoms – the debilitating process of petty persecutions, loss of a job and of public regard. Permanent house arrest, for example, is an effective way of denying a victim that public witness which gives martyrdom its earthly impact.

Modern despots do not play good-natured games with their opponents. It is hard to imagine Hitler or Stalin, Pol Pot or Saddam Hussein worrying at the prospect of a passive resister like Gandhi starving himself to death. The Mahatma was fortunate in having in the British Raj not a ruthless dictator but a bumbling, well-meaning overlord that was secretly rather fond of him. He was able to make press statements from his cell, pleading his case to the world. In the sight of God, those who die for their faith may shine brighter than the stars of heaven, but unknown martyrdoms make poor political beacon lights.

And yet, every martyr confronts the state with the realization that it cannot exact an ultimate loyalty whatever it does; there is in the humblest life an area of inner freedom that the state has no power to restrict.

In Britain at present most of this is a matter of theoretical debate, but it has been given urgency by the advent of the suicide bomber not just as a lone warrior but in whole battalions. There have been over 600 suicide bombings in Iraq. And it is being done in the name of Allah. Some Muslim scholars say that this is a gross libel. Islam is a religion of peace, and suicide bombing is contrary to the tenets of the Qur'an. But, as with the Bible, verses of the Qur'an can be quoted to prove anything.

Sam Harris, in *The End of Faith*, makes an observation some Christians will find shocking. 'Suicide bombing, in the Muslim world at least, is an explicitly religious phenomenon that is inextricable from notions of martyrdom and *jihad*, predictable on their basis, and sanctified by their logic. It is no more a secular activity than prayer.'[2]

Suicide bombing 'no more a secular activity than prayer' – it is not only in the Muslim world that the theological arguments rage and are translated into bloody actions. We in the West are part of this devils' stew of religion and politics, imperialism and freedom struggle. So we too have some hard theological thinking to do.

---

2 Harris, *The End of Faith*, p. 251.

Making Poverty History

In spite of the fact that intelligence reports say that Islamic terrorists are, in general, not down-trodden Third World peasant types but well-educated and middle class, it is commonly assumed that there is a clear link between international terrorism and world poverty. President Bush has drawn this moral – 'We fight against poverty because hope is an answer to terror.' In fairness, he sees the battle against world poverty not just as an anti-terrorist strategy but also as a challenge to his nation's compassion. He has announced a 50 per cent increase in the aid budget and has earmarked substantial funds to combat AIDs and HIV in the poor world. Many other governments and institutions including churches and personalities have joined the crusade, one of whose mottos is 'Making Poverty History' – a phrase which is highly evocative even though it does not bear grammatical analysis. Africa's parlous plight was high on the G8 world leaders' summit in Balmoral and Bob Geldof once more marshalled his legions of pop stars to entertain huge crowds throughout the world to focus popular attention on the continent.

What could be a clearer Christian imperative than duty to the disadvantaged of the earth? President Bush's Bible class will undoubtedly find many references to the poor in the Scriptures, but the picture that emerges is more complicated than will encourage a romantic perception of God's unqualified identification with them.

The Bible has the capacity to surprise, even shock us. Take, for example, our automatic assumption of the virtue of the poor. Because our consciences are seared by the gulf between our affluence and the shocking poverty of the majority of humanity, we have an almost masochistic urge to see poverty as such a cosmic enormity that those who suffer from it are beyond moral judgement; they will by right inherit a heavenly kingdom even if they do not live to be among the meek who will inherit the earth.

In fact, a closer reading of the Bible shows that every social group has its distinctive sins. The sins of the rich may thunder for retribution – greed, complacency, power-hunger and blindness to the claims of justice, yet there are also the whispering sins of the poor – envy, resentment and defensive viciousness – amply excusable in the sense that were we to share their plight we would behave fifty times worse. Nevertheless, the crime in the festering slum or overcrowded refugee camp is evidence that even the barest existence cannot, by definition, be sinless. Of course, it is easier to imagine God exercising his prerogative of mercy in favour of the hungry peasant who is little more than skin and bones than towards the cigar-puffing capitalist in a shiny Rolls-Royce. But a whole theology cannot be constructed out of one's emotions, however deeply felt.

The cup of water given or withheld which is the point of Jesus' parable of the sheep and the goats may have great significance in determining one's spiritual destiny (Matthew 25.31–46), but it cannot constitute a comprehensive doctrine of salvation. In the scales of God, social injustice does not weigh exactly with damnation, though it must exert considerable pressure on the balance. To put it starkly and even cruelly, can the whole scheme of redemption depend upon a historical contingency, the economic plight of humanity at one point in time?

In only one parable does Jesus deal specifically with the relationship between the rich and the poor – the story of Dives and Lazarus (Luke 16.19–31). It doesn't offer any solution to the spiritual plight of the hungry in either global or personal terms. Indeed, of all the parables, its meaning seems to be most opaque, except at the most obvious level where it must be assumed that anyone impervious to the plight of the poor with a Bible in his hand and Lazarus at his door is beyond the sanctions of hell or the blandishments of heaven. But this is my righteous indignation asserting itself: that is not what the parable says.

We have some excuse for misunderstanding the parable because of the wide currency given to its popular title, 'Dives and Lazarus'. In fact, the Gospel in which it is recorded makes no mention of the name 'Dives' which is simply the Latin for a rich man. So it is the story of an anonymous rich man and a beggar who *is* named, though his name 'Lazarus' – 'He whom God helps' – sounds like a sick joke. If Lazarus is an example of those whom God helps, then God help those he doesn't!

Lazarus has a name, and little else. It is the only way of distinguishing him from millions of his kind, ragged, stinking, ulcerous. The rich man has no name because he needs none. His possessions are his means of identification, though they don't constitute an identity. He has an address to which accounts might be sent, and no doubt a luxurious mode of transport that draws attention to his every movement. In the daily commerce of living, it is enough. As every confidence trickster knows, you can drive up to a posh store in a Rolls and walk out loaded with good things on the strength of an undecipherable signature.

The parable is about what it means to have everything and yet nothing. This is the luxury of the rich, their every whim is met before it has formed itself into a desire. This is why Jesus warned them they would have a hard time getting into the kingdom of heaven; not because they are necessarily nasty types; on the contrary, many of them are good people, but they have been so conditioned to expect a cheque book to open most of the doors in this life, they tend to make the dangerous assumption that the gates of the kingdom will swing apart at the flourish of a golden pen.

In its human aspect, the kingdom of God is a network of mutual dependency. And that is a currency in which many of the rich are deficient. They never discover their true poverty – not lack of what they need but who they need. So when the rich man dies, Jesus sketches out the dimensions of his peculiar anguish in a couple of sentences. He burns with objectless desire. He is a raging torrent of undirected passion. Like Stone Age man in a supermarket, he doesn't know what to ask for. His actual request is as pathetic as it is trivial, water to cool his tongue. It would never occur to him to ask for a miracle, release from torment. That might just be granted to him, for a miracle is an event far beyond one's expectations. And this man has always lived to the limit of his expectations. The way out into the kingdom is barred to him, for the kingdom is for the desperate who know that only a miracle can save them.

Which brings us to Lazarus, who is utterly vulnerable. He suffers the scorn of the strong, the obliviousness of the rich, the ravages of the weather. As a detail in the story makes clear, he lacks even the strength to brush aside the dogs licking at his sores. Yet when he can make the effort, he has the shamelessness of the beggar. He has no false pride, he cannot afford the luxury of self-respect and will grovel in the dust for a coin or a crust of bread. This is why Lazarus has a name. He is humanity, *in extremis*, no doubt; humanity when all its posturings and pretensions have been stripped away. He is the raw material of the kingdom because he knows that only a daily miracle can save him.

The parable of Dives and Lazarus is not about judgement. The description of the fate of each man after death is not a warning about what the greedy rich and the helpless poor can expect when they fall into God's hands. Jesus is not drawing awesome conclusions about the nature of eternal life; the story is not a lens through which we can glimpse the beyond, it is a mirror that throws back an image of the here and now.

Jean-Paul Sartre wrote, 'Hell is other people.' That's a half truth; heaven, too, is other people. Lazarus' poverty puts him at the mercy of virtually anybody, and that, however, degrading, is a form of relationship. Note how beggars congregate on benches in the city centre or round the fires of refugee camps; they have a desperate gregariousness. Dives' wealth cuts him off from his fellow human beings, so he knows neither heaven nor hell; just a limbo of which he is the sole occupant. According to the Book of Genesis, God in giving Eve to Adam as a companion said, 'It is not good that the man should be alone' (2.18). Isolation and aloneness set human beings against each other not in friendly rivalry but deadly competitiveness. The Hindu holy book, *The Bhagavagita*, says 'Hell has three gates: lust, anger and greed.' Those are the egotistical sins, sins of personal assertiveness.

Dives is innately decent and asks if his brothers might be warned of his fate, and he gets the bleak reply, 'They have Moses and the prophets.' But Moses and the prophets talked about people, about relationships, a foreign language to Dives and his ilk. Nor would someone returning from the dead get them to mend their ways. For that would be a miracle and they live in a world of rock-solid facts.

This story must not be invoked to baptize the present economic status quo. Because the grinding poverty of Lazarus makes him a true member of the human race by forcing on him dependence and vulnerability, this is no argument against engaging in the struggle to make poverty history. It is a declaration that economic justice is not an end in itself but a means of increasing the number and variety of human contacts; to provide the things needful, and only the things needful, for enriching relationships.

If there is a link between poverty and terrorism, then massive aid or even a transformation of the global economy will not in themselves sever it. It is not just the West's financial dealings with the poor world that need reforming; it has a god which needs toppling, the god of the Dives of this world – the Market. Note how the press and commentators refer to it as though it were a living being – the Market is 'happy' or 'sceptical' or 'nervous'. In Old Testament times, the people feared Yahweh's reaction to what they had done. These days it is the Market whose verdict is awaited with anxiety. It has the attributes of a traditional deity; it is all-powerful. Even the Communists couldn't beat it. It outlasted them and now flourishes in the ruins of their regimes. And the Market as God is omnipresent, it is everywhere, turning the whole of creation into a commodity. It dominates every area of life. For instance, traditional religions have regarded human beings as sacred, but long ago the Market reduced them to an inventory of spare parts to be sold a piece at a time – blood, sperm, fertilizable eggs, and no doubt human genes will soon be added. And if in spite of having bought a spanking new body you are still unhappy, the Market can sell you peace of mind and personal fulfilment offered by some psychological guru or life-style consultant.

Just like the Christian God, the Market loves sinners. You can commit criminal acts on an epic scale, and when they let you out of gaol, there will be someone at the gates with a cheque book, because everything is for sale, even your secrets and your reputation. It has turned celebrity or notoriety into a form of currency.

The Market God is insatiable: its motto is 'there is never enough'. So the struggle between the West and the rest is at root a theological as well as an economic issue – it is a clash of gods. For one lesson all the great religions teach is that the secret of living in harmony with creation is in knowing just how much is enough. How much do we need for the good life? If religion cannot get that message across to the rich nations, then future generations are going to inherit a bleak world.

The Moral Foundations of
Political Life

If President Bush and the British Prime Minister are to be believed, the democratic way of life is under threat from international terrorism. Draconian security measures will not in the end guarantee our survival; militarily strong societies rarely collapse from external threats. Like rotten trees they are likely to fall because they have been eaten away from inside. Indeed, Al Qa'eda has declared that it is at war against the West because of its materialism and spiritual bankrupcy.

Our survival may depend on a rediscovery of the moral values on which our society was built, a re-assertion of our essential genius. A good starting point for looking at this issue is Lady Thatcher's notorious statement, 'There is no such thing as society.' Her favourite economist, F. H. Hayek, spelt it out in pseudo-biblical terms. He wrote: 'An order in which everyone treated his neighbour as himself would be one where comparatively few would be fruitful and multiply.' He doesn't go on to say what the consequences would be of treating one's neighbour as an enemy – a policy likely to prove fruitful only in multiplying mayhem. But here is the battle line drawn not between alternative political policies or economic doctrines but between fundamental philosophies of life.

Mrs Thatcher's dictum could be countered by another which

128

William Morris, the great turn-of-the-century socialist, put into the mouth of John Ball, the rebel priest of Blackheath: 'Fellowship is heaven and lack of fellowship is hell.' Fellowship is a venerable word; it has become rather churchy, but its roots go deep in the Bible. The more extreme feminists might find a hint of sexism in it, but there is no comparable term which has such rich historical associations and resonances. It speaks of the essential need of human beings for mutual comfort and encouragement, protection and development. Fellowship shields us in our vulnerability and finds expression for our interdependence; it reinforces our strengths and neutralizes our weaknesses, for none of us in isolation has all the gifts and graces needful for the completely fulfilling life.

Fellowship celebrates the truth that the things human beings have in common are much more fundamental than those which divide them – there are no places at the Feast of Fellowship reserved for guests of a particular class, colour, sex or religion; all are welcome to sit down and eat. It is a feast – and much of the battle is to ensure there is food for all, but it is also a feast in the sense that there is room for celebration, play and laughter as well as work and serious talk and political striving. We may tend our garden or say our prayers, kick a ball or paint a portrait. All human activities have validity so long as they do not diminish someone else's life chances.

Fellowship is not threatened but enhanced by the rich diversity of human interests and preoccupations. It is not the grim uniformity of a congregation of ants in a heap or bees in a hive where bodies jostle but souls are alone. Whereas in a collectivism, individuals are submerged like uniform cells in a quivering mass, where true fellowship exists, they are valued because the goal of real community is the enlargement and cultivation of the individual life.

'Fellowship is heaven,' said William Morris. Alan Bennett defined heaven as Matlock in the Sky. Fellowship grows like Matlock, a community with an identity, distinctive accents and social quirks; it is not welded together like a vast machine. After all, the most elaborate social mechanism of modern times, in Russia and Eastern Europe, recently came clanking to a halt, and out of every sprung rivet hole issued an explosive mixture of the spirits it sought to extinguish – nationalism, political nonconformity and religion. True fellowship can contain such forces – not easily, not without hazard, for they generate passionate feelings and fierce partisanship – but their legitimate claims can be harmonized. Democracy stands or falls by this conviction.

True fellowship is heaven in the sense that individuals can only achieve their full potential in a setting of social harmony. But as William Morris warned, lack of fellowship is hell. For all but a small number of intensely creative people, solitariness is pathological, psychologically crippling and spiritually debilitating, economically wasteful and morally undermining. If human beings do not care for one another in a community, they will end up preying on one another in a jungle.

It would be naïve to imagine that fellowship is easily attainable. There are powerful forces in human nature tending towards self-centredness and greed which must be mastered by painful struggle. And there are powers at work in the world which are quite outside human control and affect our life chances, call them fate, destiny or providence. So we are not in the business of trying to create perfection on earth; that has been tried, and every brave Utopian experiment has foundered on the rocks of harsh reality. Perfection is beyond our reach, but not the more modest goal of extending throughout human life the areas where kindness, consideration and co-operation rule, and harsh competitiveness is checked if not banished.

How do we do it? What are the moral values that undergird and sustain the politics of fellowship? One of Jesus' sayings can be translated from the Greek in either of two ways: 'the kingdom of God is *within* you' or 'the kingdom of God is *among* you'. Both interpretations would be equally apt. The moral good is both an inner force and a social goal.

I believe there are a number of primary moral values; 'primary' in the sense that they are the minimal moral foundations of the fully human life. And they are self-evident in the sense that we cannot go behind them to get at even more basic values on which they rest. Like Euclid's propositions in geometry, we can 'see' that they are true. If we want to do geometry we have to take Euclid on trust. If we wish to live the civilized, humane life, we will take these values on trust and honour them. Believers might call them revealed truths, they have been given to us, and our experience confirms them.

In no particular order: there is *justice* which is concerned with the boundaries between individuals in the community. We cannot live together without some rules. No worthwhile common activity is possible unless we can harmonize our claims on others and theirs on us. Justice is about keeping my self-assertiveness in check so that it conflicts as little as possible with yours. It defines how we should behave not simply towards those we love, like or find congenial, but towards those we happen to be thrown against by chance or a common destiny; even how we should behave towards our enemies. Justice is the hard skeleton which gives shape to community life, the framework within which fellowship can blossom.

Being human, we are all vulnerable, capable of coming to harm because we will always be to some extent at the mercy of others, so there has to be some kind of agreement which limits the damage we can do to each other; a compact backed by the sanction of the law. And this compact is universal in the sense that it cannot be restricted to one group, nation, sex, class or race. For where there is injustice anywhere, sooner or later it will fetch up on our doorstep in resentment and instability, an explosive mixture that robs all of us of the good life.

The Christian faith takes a generous though realistic view of the average person's capacity for justice. It assumes tolerable decency as a general human characteristic. The vast majority of people are neither angels nor devils. Not being angels, they are prone to put their own interests first, so power enters the equation as the measure of coercion necessary to see that others also get their due. But they are not devils either. They are capable of fellowship. They have the will and desire to settle most disputes by mutual consent and peaceful adjudication. It must be assumed that they can be trusted with freedom.

Justice is oblivious of the power, wealth and wisdom of those who seek it, though there is one overriding consideration. Any inequality in the distribution of social values must be exercised in favour of the less advantaged. This was a central theme of the Old Testament prophets, who insisted the widow, the poor and the orphan were dear to God's heart. In the words of Micah: 'He has told you, O mortal, what is good . . . to do justice, and to love kindness, and to walk humbly with your God' (6.8). That is a sublime summary of the way the just life is crowned by mercy and humility.

The Bible's view of justice, as thundered forth by the prophets, is nothing like so simple and cogent as Aristotle's, 'to each his due!' The snag with that definition is that I am always alert to circumstances in which I get less than my due, but I may not be equally sensitive to the fact that you are being given less than your due. The prophets declaimed that God was angry with princes and kings because they turned away the poor from their doors. Biblical justice always has a built-in bias towards the poor of the earth – as Moffatt's translation puts it, 'He has torn imperial powers from their thrones, but the humble have been lifted high.'

Besides justice, *truth* is to be prized as the capacity to bring one's thinking and feeling into agreement with the reality of the world outside; to value whatever comes our way at its proper worth. Truth usually presents itself practically as common sense, that instinctive wisdom based not only on our own experience but on the accumulated experience of humanity at large. From time immemorial it has kept us in touch with reality – 'pull the other one!' we say with brisk common sense when confronted by the bizarre or the plainly nonsensical.

This common sense capacity to get to the root of the matter and tell it like it is, as the Americans say, cannot be too highly prized in a society which is adept at self-delusion; which puts unpleasant things in fancy wrappings and gives pretty names to ugly realities – which talks of aid when it means fraud, development when it means exploitation, incentives when it means greed and Victorian values when it means Darwinian survival of the fittest.

Truth is advanced by competition among ideas. Bertrand Russell wrote, 'In matters of opinion it is a good thing if there is a vigorous discussion between different schools of thought. In the mental world there is everything to be said in favour of a struggle for existence, leading with luck to the survival of the fittest.'

And the quest for truth demands constant openness to the possibility that we are in error. You could call it humility before the truth or tolerance; it amounts to the same thing. Three hundred years ago, Oliver Cromwell when Lord Protector wrote to our Puritan forebears pleading for tolerance towards the Irish. He used a phrase which became immortal, 'I beseech you, consider in the bowels of God that you may be mistaken.' All those who love democracy are engaged in a twofold, paradoxical task. We must struggle against intolerance in all its forms and still believe in our hearts that we may just be mistaken.

Humility before the truth or tolerance means accepting that that there is no infallibility in human life. We must be prepared to explain and defend our positions and if they prove indefensible, admit we were wrong and try again. Unless society is to be blown all over the place by the gales of a public opinion notorious for its fickleness, there has got to be a point at which people stop messing around with the truth, spinning it, polishing it, shading it, where it ceases to be negotiable, up for grabs for the most powerful, the cleverest, the slickest-tongued to manipulate.

The Bible treats truth in a special sense in order to respond to the question, 'How can we become free?' The answer is knowledge of a special kind, saving knowledge – 'you will know the truth, and the truth will make you free' (John 8.32). This truth which human beings must know in order to free themselves is not the truth about religion or the teaching of Jesus. It is neither doctrinal truth nor any body of knowledge about holy things. The truth which frees is Jesus Christ himself. There is a daring verb in John 3.21: 'Those who *do* what is true come to the light.' It means participating in the very being of the one who is the truth, and therefore it is as dynamic as he is. This truth is not something that lies dormant in our minds; it changes things. In the words of Paul Tillich: 'Truth is the stream of life centred in Jesus Christ, actualized in anybody who is connected with him, organized in the assembly of God, the Church.'[1]

Besides justice and truth, *freedom* is to be cherished. This is the belief that human life has a value in itself, so human beings should not be used for purposes alien to their essential dignity; indeed, no human being should be used at all. It is easiest to define freedom by simply negating the word in common speech – to be free is not to be bound or constrained or caged or enslaved. To be free is to be able to express spontaneously our own nature; to be our best selves. Freedom is not just a restraint on arbitrary power but a good in itself, which bequeaths on human beings all those qualities necessary for the development of a fulfilled and responsible personality.

Human freedom demands not merely free individuals but the relationship of free people; in a word, fellowship. The core of human freedom lies in our capacity to be ourselves for other people. If we want an example of what it means to be free, what it

---

1 Paul Tillich, *The New Being*, SCM Press, 1956, p. 72.

feels like in experience, we must think of the occasions when we have found ourselves totally spontaneous and unconstrained in the company of family or friends; we were completely ourselves and completely free. That is the fellowship ideal. It is an ideal impossible of entire fulfilment in the wider community, but all the cumbersome apparatus of government and politics exists to encourage that spirit rather than to repress it.

Of course, there is no such thing as absolute liberty in the real world; only free choices within one set of limitations or another. If I have a pencil in my hand, I can draw a circle or a square or any other shape. That is my right, that is what liberty means. But I cannot make a thing that is both a circle, a square and some other shape at the same time. Nor can I produce an unlimited square or an unconfined circle. I must abide by the limitations of the non-contradictory. Thus, no rational human being feels a sense of deprivation if he or she is not given the freedom to commit murder or to drive on whichever side of the road may take his or her fancy. The obedient are not unfree so long as they are able to recognize the sanity, rationality and wisdom of the rules they are required to observe. As G. K. Chesterton warned, when you break big laws, you don't get liberty; you don't even get anarchy, you get small laws.

Implicit in freedom is equality, because freedom cannot exist in the presence of special privileges or where the rights of some depend on the pleasure of others. I would wish to qualify the word 'equality' and talk about moral equality, for it is obvious that in terms of physical strength, mental endowment, natural talent and wealth, human beings are not equal. The American Declaration of Independence does not assert that all men are equal; it says they were 'created' equal. There is a necessary denial of unlimited rights here. No one is entitled to use physical strength to tyrannize the weak, or material wealth to dispossess the poor, or superior guile to dupe the simple. Nor is equality of treatment enough where people differ in their wants, needs and condition.

My claim upon the resources and protection of the community is not equal to that of the frail, the aged and the disadvantaged. This bias in favour of those who are not economically and socially productive because of handicap may not make sense to Professor Hayek and the stern Marketeers but it is what is meant by moral equality.

Religiously, it is the destiny of every human being to be allowed by God to be free in order to know faith, hope and love, which are the three abiding realities of the life of the Spirit. We are not compelled to believe, we are allowed to, and therefore must be free in order to be able to say Yes or No to God, to choose Christ or Anti-Christ.

We are offered an infallible test of freedom. Does what purports to be freedom take us nearer to the truth, increase the possibility of our believing, hoping and loving; does it make it easier for us to follow the way of Christ?

The passion for justice, respect for the truth, the urge to be free and the right to moral equality are expressions of primary values. So is *courage*. To be courageous is to be someone on whom reliance can be placed, and hence, it is an essential ingredient in fellowship. In a sense, it is an acid test of fellowship. If someone says he or she has great concern and affection for others but is unwilling to risk unpopularity or harm on their behalf, it casts doubt on the genuineness of any protestations of friendship.

There is no worthwhile human activity which does not involve some degree of risk – physical, emotional or moral. All the great life choices are hazardous, whether of a partner, a career, a political destiny or a religious vision. To realize our full stature, we must defy things that terrify us and break a lance against opponents who seem to outmatch us. To live always within the margins of safety is the recipe for a dull life as well as an unproductive one.

For our human potential to blossom, we need a cause greater than ourselves; one that will not exhaust itself before we exhaust ourselves. There are none so sad as those who have outlived the causes to which they dedicated their lives. They linger like the rusting equipment of some long-abandoned experiment, awaiting ghostly commands to start up again that never come.

All great causes are hazardous; we might risk everything and lose. This life is fraught with all kinds of baleful possibilities which are totally unpredictable, perils round the next bend, hammer blows of fate that strike fortuitously. We cannot know how things will turn out when we embark on a course; we can only have faith. What we thought was indubitable truth may prove to be error, our celestial city is revealed as a mirage, our vision a hallucination.

There is no more practical or effectual way of showing our concern and care for others than our willingness to risk harm or danger on their behalf. The most obvious examples are members of the armed forces or police who put their lives at risk on our behalf, but there are also subtler forms of hazard to do with suffering for one's convictions or putting job and home and social position on the line in order to stand four-square for things in the best long-term interests of society, even when society itself thinks differently.

To be courageous is to be someone who will not quit the field at the sound of the first shot, who will stand firm in loyalty through good days and ill. So, courage is closely allied to constancy or integrity. We must have the constancy to live invariably by the moral values we prize – yesterday, today and tomorrow, in all possible circumstances, applying them indiscriminately to our roles in life as fathers, mothers, husbands, wives, neighbours and citizens; otherwise they are not virtues but tactics. It is courage which guarantees consistency in moral behaviour. Without courage, all other virtues are impotent; without courage, personal life is not worth the candle.

Finally, there is *love*. A professor at the University of Sussex has published a book in which he describes his search for a theory of everything – a mathematical formula summarizing all we can know about measurable reality, a few symbols that describe the totality of physical life in the universe. Christianity too has a theory of everything expressed in the stark formula: God is love. Every aspect and doctrine of the Christian faith can be derived from it: faith is divine love recognized; hope is divine love's triumph foreshadowed; revelation is divine love doing a new thing; conversion is divine love given best; salvation is divine love at peace, and so on.

That's all very well for our personal lives but what relevance might it have to the hectic world of politics and international relations? Well, the root of many of our problems as a society is not to be found in the technicalities of politics or economics but in a lack of mutual respect and trust among its members. It is easy to look at others without actually seeing them. We see a stereotype, an oversimplified image of them which is shaped by our prejudices and ignorance. Love gives us the power of imagination to put ourselves in someone else's shoes and see how our actions look from the other side of the tracks, south of the equator or on the wrong side of the breadline.

These moral values span the great monotheistic religions; indeed, they have helped to evolve and shape them in accordance with the genius of their particular revelation and teaching. But as Alastair MacIntyre points out in *After Virtue*, there have been more modern attempts to list the moral foundations of our common life. The novelist Jane Austin had, in C. S. Lewis' opinion, a profoundly moral vision and she put great store on what she called constancy and amiability; Benjamin Franklin produced a list of 13 virtues, including chastity, cleanliness, silence, industry and thrift.[2]

Whether we turn to the New Testament or to more recent moralists for guidance, there is a surprising degree of consistency

---

2 Alastair MacIntyre, *After Virtue: A Study in Moral Theory*, Duckworth, 1987, p. 185.

about what constitutes our moral obligation towards others and therefore sketches out the dimensions of the good life. Accepting that there is truth in Osama bin Laden's charge about a spiritual vacuum at the heart of the West, unless we wish it to be filled with his poisonous ideology, these classical virtues need to be revisited urgently and asserted not just by governments and political parties or the great institutions of state, but at the level of the daily cut and thrust of living in family, school and workplace.

The Doom Sayers

There are significant numbers of Christians who view the present crisis from a very special angle. They see within and beyond the violence, war and disruption hints that biblical predictions about the end of the world may be on the brink of fulfilment. Their proof text is Mark 13 and they sweep aside scholastic doubts about whether that particular section of the Gospel known as the Little Apocalypse is authentic or was added later when many of the events prophesied had actually happened. To them, what is written there is plain gospel truth. The present state of our society matches the terrible catalogue of natural disasters and human catastrophes which Jesus describes in that passage – battles, earthquakes, famines, a darkened sun and falling stars and false prophets misleading the terrified people.

Such sects as the Seventh Day Adventists and Jehovah's Witnesses live with a constant sense of urgency; the End of the World is at hand and may supervene at any moment, a thought that rarely impinges on the consciousness of most mainstream Christians. Indeed, on this issue, Christians seem to divide out into two camps. There are those who rarely think about the end and those who rarely think about anything else.

Most mainstream Christians expect things to go on in much the same way for years to come. They build ever bigger barns and plaster ecclesiastical insurance policies all over the real estate of the kingdom, but they must also recite the Apostles'

Creed – 'He shall come again in glory to judge both the quick and the dead'; sing Advent hymns – 'Lo, he comes with clouds descending'; and read whole sections of the New Testament that proclaim in one form or another the stark message, 'The end is nigh!'

We do all this with our fingers firmly crossed, because our crowded engagement diaries belie any sense that the world is about to be turned upside down. Sceptics might say that when the Pope and the Archbishop of Canterbury stop booking engagements for years ahead, this will be proof they know something of God's intentions denied to the rest of us.

It is hard to deny that these millennial sects are closer to the mind-set of primitive Christianity than the mainstream churches are. And one can neither refute nor confirm their convictions from the New Testament itself. Jesus was little short of tantalizing in what he says about the end of the world. In one place in the Gospels he hints that the end is rapidly approaching, yet he also tells stories about mustard seed and wheat and weeds which imply the kingdom will evolve according to the laws of natural growth rather than arrive suddenly; but then on yet another occasion he warns, 'But about that day or hour no one knows, neither the angels in heaven, nor the Son, but only the Father' (Mark 13.32). It is clear that it was not the date of the end but the certainty and suddenness of it which preoccupied him. But nowhere in the Gospels is there even the hint of a time-scale for the Christian enterprise that might encompass 2,000 years and stretch on into a third millennium.

When I worked at the headquarters of the BBC in Portland Place in London, most days as I walked up from Oxford Circus tube station I was confronted by an elderly gentleman bearing a placard reading 'The End is Nigh!' This was obviously his full-time occupation. Every day, come wind, come weather, he tramped the streets of the West End, shrugging off the good natured mockery of passers by, waving his placard in the air, virtually thrusting it in the faces of those who sought to hurry past him with averted gaze.

Doom saying is a venerable trade which goes way back into the past and enjoyed a renaissance recently when the Millennium in 2000 approached. Members of a number of sects were convinced that they were coming up to the finishing post at midnight on 31 December 1999 and prepared themselves. In the event, they were mistaken, but shrugging off the jeers of the cynics, they went back to the Scriptures, most notably to Daniel and the Book of Revelation, did their sums again and arrived at a revised date for the end in the light of which they now live, still keenly expectant.

In fact, intense expectancy runs as an undertone through much of the New Testament. Just as Thessalonian Christians stood around in groups neglecting their work awaiting Christ's return, so believers in Corinth, though Greeks, seem to have used the Aramaic invocation, 'Even so, Lord, come!' as a code or a password; in Paul's Letter to the Romans, Christ's glorious return is the unspoken assumption behind great tracts of his reasoning, and there are echoes of the doctrine in non-Pauline writings such as the Pastoral Epistles and Hebrews. In the Second Letter of Peter, the time-scale slips somewhat, a thousand years are to be considered a mere day in the eyes of God so that as many sinners as possible might repent before the Lord's glorious return. The Bible's final book, the Revelation of St John the Divine contains a series of visions of the end.

Ironically, while the mainstream churches have abandoned doom saying, the practice has been been taken up enthusiastically by some political theorists, economists and scientists. Some years ago, Lord Rees-Mogg, former editor of *The Times*, wrote an article entitled, 'Is this the end of life as we know it?' In it, he claimed that if we are lucky, humanity has about 50 years left. 'Most of the graphs of human development, population, ecology, technology, nuclear proliferation and the spread of disease are on an explosive curve. The lines shoot off the graph somewhere in the middle of the next century.'

Some scientists are also warning about the possibility of catastrophe. There are predictions that the earth will be reduced to a burnt-out cinder by the sun either cooling or else exploding and engulfing us in a cosmic holocaust. And if by any chance we should escape that big bang there's a mammoth asteroid already hurtling through space and expected to collide with our planet in the not too distant future. According to Dr Brian Marsden of the Harvard-Smithsonian Institute for Astrophysics, the most favoured date is 14 August 2126. A similar collision between the earth and an asteroid 65 million years ago is believed to have triggered a nuclear winter which wiped out the dinosaurs and most other forms of life on earth. Dr Marsden thinks that next time the asteroid, whose pet name is Smith-Tuttle after two of the people who first spotted it in 1862, will do the job properly.

There is a real irony here. While many Christians have lost any sense of apocalyptic urgency, the secular society around them has become increasingly prone to fears of imminent cataclysm. The West's mood has degenerated from smugness to bafflement in a few decades. The society that split the atom and landed on the moon confesses itself utterly confounded by problems that seem to admit of no solutions – rising crime rates, the irresistible decline of the traditional family, mass starvation, dangerous fluctuations in scarce commodities, tribal, racial and religious conflicts, irreversible environmental damage, and now terror attacks. Great yawning gulfs have opened up where once there was solid ground in politics, morality and spirituality.

In December 1992, the then newly elected President of the United States, Bill Clinton, called together over a hundred leading economists, financiers and industrial leaders in a seminar to address the country's economic crisis. After five days the President admitted in exasperation that not only were the experts hopelessly at odds about the way forward, they couldn't even agree what the problem was. Hence, there is around a kind of street-level apocalyptic which says in effect, 'Something's got to happen; things can't go on like this.'

But the gentleman with the placard bearing the legend 'The End is Nigh' is on quite different ground from the scientific or economic doom forecasters. I doubt he knows or cares much about Lord Rees-Mogg's statistical projections or Dr Marsden's scientific forecasts even though they appear to give his stark announcement credibility. He derives his burning sense of urgency about the end not from any body of human knowledge but from his understanding of God's will as spelt out in the Bible. How God sorts things out is a matter of supreme indifference to the placard carrier. His single theme is that the world is about to dissolve into terminal chaos so people had better make their peace with God while there is still time.

Many Christians find this sort of thing very embarrassing. It's quite fashionable to prophesy that the world will come to an end if we don't do something about such issues as global warming and overpopulation. That's good green thinking, and we can practise what we preach by using biologically friendly detergents and recycling empty bottles. But to suggest that God might, at any moment, bring the curtain down on history in a grand apocalyptic denouement is an idea as disconcerting as it is strange.

Throughout Christian history, individuals and groups have sought to go further than the New Testament ventured, read the mind of God and put an exact time and place to the return of Christ in glory. Sometimes, political motives underlay such prediction; thus, one reason given for the Crusades was that Christendom must regain control of the Holy Land before the Lord's return. At the close of twelfth century, Joachim of Floris did his sums from the Book of Revelation and announced that the year 1260 was the date of Christ's return because 1260 days is mentioned in Revelations 12.6. He saw in contemporary events signs of the end, the aggression of the Saracens, the Crusades, the rise of the monasteries. When he incurred the wrath of the Pope, he adroitly claimed that one sure sign of the end was the animosity of the papacy to one of God's true prophets. The great Bible translator William Wyclif also thought the corruption of the papacy was a portent of the end.

J. A. Bengel, the eighteenth-century Lutheran scholar, whose commentaries John Wesley much admired and translated, announced that the millennium would arrive in 1836 followed by 1,000 years before the end. In America, the Shakers; in Germany, the People of God; in nineteenth-century Britain, Edward Irving the Scottish Presbyterian – all looked to the imminent end of the world. The Plymouth Brethren also came into being around this time dedicated to restoring purity of Christian life in time for Christ's return.

It is easy to sneer at these sects, but however mistakenly, they minister to humanity's hunger for hope. They live with a sense of urgent expectation which fuels their missionary drive. They indefatigably trudge the streets, knocking on doors and trying to warn everyone who will give them a hearing about the wrath to come.

The doom sayer's bald announcement reminds the mainstream churches of a historical embarrassment they prefer to forget. Quite simply, the Second Coming did not come. As it moves on, the New Testament dramatically highlights the problem. The circle of believers who might be privileged to behold Christ's glorious return is narrowed by degrees. At first all Christians could hope for it in their lifetime – 'There are some standing here who will not taste death before they see the kingdom of God.' Then it is promised to 'some'. Finally, in the closing chapter of John's Gospel there is guarded reference to the beloved disciple; Jesus says, 'If it is my will that he remain until I come, what is that to you?' (21.22) There is a medieval legend based on this text that St John lingered on, over 1,000 years old, in a remote Middle-Eastern monastery, waiting for Jesus to fulfil his promise and take him off to glory.

Jesus warned his disciples, 'Stay awake, be alert,' but human nature being what it is, believers cannot live indefinitely on a knife-edge of breathless expectancy, with their bags mentally packed. They will inevitably revert to normality. As Jesus elsewhere predicted, they will spend their time 'as in the days of Noah . . . eating and drinking, marrying and giving in marriage' (Luke 17.26; Matthew 24.27). How could it be otherwise? People would go stark raving mad if they had to live constantly at the level of spiritual and psychological intensity appropriate to an ultimate crisis. Therefore because the end was indefinitely delayed, an alternative strategy of worldly witness and service was taken up by the early Church and became the driving force of Christian mission. Mainstream Christians began to hold to that aspect of the Advent doctrine which speaks of the risen Christ in the power of the Holy Spirit intervening in normal events, not to bring history to an end some time in the future but to seek to change it as it wears on.

For doom sayers, worldly pessimism is the only realistic Christian attitude. Yet however grim the outlook, the prognostications of the 'When things get bad enough God will stop the show' school, though understandable, have got to be mistaken; otherwise the whole point of creation would be frustrated. It would be the ultimate confession of divine failure if human greed, arrogance, stupidity and sheer wickedness could determine the outcome of history and the timing of the end.

It is hard to reconcile that passage in Mark 13 with the drift of the Bible generally. At the very outset, in the Book of Genesis, there is a ringing declaration that God's creation in its nature and purpose is good. And throughout the Old Testament there runs the thread of trust in God's providential care. The prophets insisted that there is a purpose in things and through good days and ill God will be faithful to it. And God's servants can trust their lives to his loving care, even in misfortune and defeat. The prophet Habakkuk declared, 'Though the fig tree does not blossom, and no fruit is on the vines; though the produce of the olive fails and the fields yield no food; though the flock is cut off from the fold and there is no herd in the stalls, yet I will rejoice in the Lord; I will exult in the God of my salvation' (3.17–18).

Nor was worldly despair the essential temper of Jesus as the one who proclaimed the nearness of the kingdom. He insisted that the earth bears perpetual and everlasting witness to the goodness of God the Father. His sun shines on good and bad alike; he cares for the falling sparrow; he loves the beauty of the flowers of the field. When Jesus exhorted his followers to turn their backs on things of the world it was not because they were inherently evil but because God could be trusted to look after them. Believers could move around in the world confident and unanxious because they were in their Father's house.

It is from the routine operations of a good world that the laws and methods of the kingdom are deduced. According to the parables of Jesus, the ploughman, the farmer, the fisherman, the merchant, busy, efficient, engaged people, embody some essential aspect of the secret kingdom. It is those who show competence in secular affairs who will be trusted with great responsibilities here-after. Folly, miscalculation, lack of foresight are as damaging in the spiritual realm as they are in worldly affairs. There is a sort of ethical continuity between two kingdoms – to write off this world is to undervalue the other.

Indeed, the Book of Revelation – regarded by millennial doom sayers as a happy hunting ground for proof of imminent catas-trophe – is a tract originally intended to be a tonic for despairing believers. Its essential message is that beyond the great set-piece battles between good and evil, a new earth as well as a new heaven will stand revealed. And this is what is distinctive about the Christian hope for the end, the belief that the final act of the drama will be played out, not in some supernatural realm beyond the skies, but down here where Jesus of Nazareth left footprints in the sand and blood on a cross.

However short or prolonged our future as a species may be,

the whole thrust of the New Testament is that it will be a divine initiative and not human sinfulness or natural catastrophe which brings the cosmic drama to a climax. It would be the ultimate confession of failure if God could not finish what he began at the creation – if things were to get so bad that he could only regain control by cutting his losses and leaving the earth to its fate. He would be like a captain having to abandon ship after managing to get some of the passengers and crew into the lifeboats, but at the price of losing the vessel. And it is the vessel – the whole creation – that is to be renewed, not just individual believers.

Though these Christian doom sayers are passionately devoted to Jesus, John the Baptist is their real role model. Like him, they warn society of the approach of the Day of the Lord, whose worst consequences can only be mitigated by a baptism of repentance. Then the saved will be spirited away from the wreckage of a world totally destroyed by human sinfulness. This is in sharp contrast to Jesus' teaching about the end. The difference is expressed in their characteristic slogans: 'The judgement of wrath is coming' or 'The kingdom of heaven is at hand'. It was the contrast between the Day of the Lord as threat and as promise. Does it cast people down in despair or set them on their feet in hope?

As the apostles pondered what Jesus had taught and done, they began to see the kingdom of God incarnate in him; message and messenger had merged. Jesus declared that everything depended on a right relationship to the kingdom; they interpreted this to mean a right relationship with him. In the Gospels the preaching is of the kingdom; in the Epistles it is of 'Jesus and him crucified'. And the Acts of the Apostles shows the transition from one to the other. For the early Church, Jesus was the clue to the meaning of the kingdom.

As the great early twentieth-century theologian Peter Forsyth put it:

The gospel of Christ replaced the gospel of the Kingdom because by his death he replaced all that the Kingdom contained. The gospel of the Kingdom was Christ in essence; Christ was the gospel of the Kingdom with power. The Kingdom was Christ in a mystery; Christ was the publication of that kingdom. He was the truth of his own greatest gospel. It is wherever he is. To have him is to ensure it.'[1]

And this assurance delivers us from vain anxiety about the future, the foretelling of which is not confined to religious sects. In the everyday, non-religious world, predicting the future used to be the business of sea-front gypsies gazing into crystal balls in tents decorated with the signs of the zodiac. Now it is a respectable science practised by academics with formidable qualifications who use the technology of the space age to construct complex models that claim to demonstrate the interaction of events yet to occur. Statistics has replaced astrology as the essential tool of the futurologist.

But had computers existed in 1875 when horse-drawn transport was universal, they would certainly have predicted that by the twenty-first century the whole world would be covered seven feet deep in horse droppings. But the trend was reversed by the invention of the internal combustion engine – Factor X, which no self-respecting computer could be expected to take account of.

There is too a Factor X at work in the realm of the Spirit, which inhibits Christians from getting too involved in futurology. In fact, they are warned against calculating times and seasons; indeed, if the New Testament is anything to go by, whenever early Christians made predictions about the future, as in the matter of the date of the end of the world, they were invariably wrong.

Christians possess no special sense denied anyone else by which to determine the shape of tomorrow. They make a more extraordinary claim, that their understanding of the future comes

---

1 Quoted in A. M. Hunter, *P. T. Forsyth*, SCM Press, 1974, p. 74.

from tomorrow. Eschatology – the study of the last things – describes a process which is the exact opposite of prediction. It is certainly a series of statements about the end, but insists that the end is not that which comes after everything else; it is not the culmination of an infinite series of historical chess moves. It is a way of looking at the present from the perspective of the future, rather like an astronaut seeing the earth from the moon.

The New Testament undermines any doctrine of futurology by insisting that except in the most impersonal sense, the future cannot be predicted. As the author of the First Epistle of John put it, 'We are God's children now; what we will be has not yet been revealed' (3.2). We are not pre-programmed robots. According to John's Gospel, 'to all . . . who believed in his name, he gave power to become' (1.12). The power to become is the gift of an open future, though we must always keep a weather-eye open for the tantalizing presence of Factor X, the totally unpredictable and unexpected. This is why Jesus counselled constant vigilance.

Christian doom sayers remind conventional believers of an often forgotten dimension of the gospel. If God is unable to bring a decisive end to what he first started, and at a moment of his choosing, then he is a minor divinity. But if he can, then logically, the moment of his choosing could just as well be tomorrow morning as 1,000 years from now.

Things Shaken, Things Unshaken

What are we to make of the turmoil of our time? There is no shortage of voices pronouncing the imminent end of Western civilization. As long ago as 1969, Sir Kenneth Clark began his trail-blazing television series *Civilization* in Paris. He was talking about the collapse of European civilization, when the barbarians sacked Rome and plunged us into the Dark Ages. 'In the last few years,' he said, 'we've developed an uneasy feeling this could happen again. And advanced thinkers have begun to ask if our civilization is worth saving.'

They could be right; no civilization lasts for ever. Arnold Toynbee in his *Study of History* described 17 civilizations that had their day and then ceased to be. In old age, he wondered whether he himself might live to see the end of yet another:

In Western Christendom till within living memory, there were still some who believed that they, in their generation, might live to see the denouement, not just of the current act, but of the play itself. I have lived to see the (Christian) belief in the certainty of the coming of 'the Last Things' fade out in the Western world, and have lived to see it become a mundane possibility that would be translated into fact by an act, not of God, but of Man. This is the reality for those who envisage the

Last Things in terms, not of theology, but of the potentialities of the misuse of atomic power for death and evil.[1]

Now in the face of such stark realities, there are two options not open to the Christian. One is to cling to a Utopian belief in progress, the conviction that things are bound slowly but surely to get better as knowledge drives out ignorance and good gradually overcomes evil. Though there may from time to time be set-backs, sharp dips on the graph line of human progress, the general thrust is onwards and upwards. Jesus demolished that doctrine in a few sharp sentences in the parable of the wheat and weeds. Wheat and weeds, good and evil, grow inseparably, nurtured by the same sun. And the more mature the wheat, the more strangulating the weeds. Within history, every extension of good opens up new possibilities of evil right up to the last moment of recorded time; right up to the harvest. So Utopianism is out.

Nor can we take refuge in apocalypse and skedaddle to the nearest mountain top, metaphorically if not literally, and await the arrival of that celestial balloon which will carry faithful believers up and away from a sad, bad world. It would be the ultimate confession of divine failure if human greed, arrogance, stupidity and sheer wickedness could determine the outcome of history. If things have got so bad that the only way God can regain control is by abandoning the whole enterprise, to what end was the life, death and resurrection of Jesus? It was the whole creation or nothing which was redeemed by Christ. When the disciples asked Jesus whether he would restore Israel to its old glory, he made it clear that he was doing a new thing, not trying to salvage what could be saved from an enterprise that had gone tragically wrong. A new heaven and a new earth was to be the ultimate consequence of God's kingly rule.

There is no biblical word which offers a way out of this, the human predicament, but there is one that points to a way

---

1 A. Toynbee, *Experiences*, Oxford University Press, 1969, pp. 370–1.

through, which speaks to the gravity of the situation. The Letter to the Hebrews was written at a time when yawning chasms seemed to be opening up under the feet of Jewish Christians who watched with despair the familiar and well-loved landmarks of the old religion being swept away: 'I will shake not only the earth but also the heaven . . . so that what cannot be shaken may remain' (Hebrews 12.26–7). They are terrifying words and yet not at odds with the spirit of Scripture as a whole. Indeed, this verse from Hebrews is an echo of the passage in Haggai (2.6) where the prophet recalls that God shook the very world to its foundation in the act of giving the Law.

They are words that encapsulate the consequences of the Jesus-event not just for personal faith nor for the Church's life but for the whole created order, the pain and poetry, the promise and judgement unleashed into history by God's intervention. They offer a clue to the way the old world is to be transformed into a new creation.

The author of the Letter to the Hebrews spells it all out in three tough propositions: *First, accept that what can be shaken, must be.*

The contrast between what is enduring and what is transient runs through many of the parables of the kingdom. The foundations of the house built on sand crumble; the wealth laid up in earthly treasure houses is ravaged by moth and rust and theft; the seed sown on stony ground is shrivelled by the sun; the talent buried in the earth proves sterile; the house swept clean and left empty ends up teeming with unwanted and destructive life. On the other hand, the house built on rock survives the storm; the seed sown in fertile ground brings forth an abundant harvest, the talent put to work fructifies.

That's all very straightforward and reassuring, but it is a much more rigorous, even paradoxical, lesson this text from Hebrews teaches. It asserts that everything that can be shaken must be – not just the bad but also the good, not just the shoddy but also the well-wrought, not just what degrades but what dignifies our humanity. For in the end, the greatest threat to our well-doing comes not from human wickedness or foolishness, though they do their damage; the great enemy is time, time as a perpetual perishing, time that undermines and weakens and ages and renders obsolete even the most worthwhile of our achievements.

This is one of the consistent themes of the Old Testament: history is an order of growing and dying, of waxing and waning, prosperity and decay – 'The grass withers, the flower fades . . . surely the people are grass,' cries Isaiah (40.7). 'The foundations of the earth vanish; they wear out like a robe,' says the Psalmist (102.26).

Generations, empires, dynasties arise, struggle, prevail, then weaken, falter and disappear. And in our arrogance, we try to stave off time's clay finger by investing our hope in institutions that are the finest fruit of our human virtuosity. Behold the wonders of our political systems; the cunning of our economic strategies; the brilliance of our technological mastery, our military prowess, our artistic genius, our religious wisdom! And so intoxicated are we by our achievements that we ignore those words uttered a long time ago by a desert prophet called Micah who warned, 'You must not worship things you have made yourself' (5.13, Moffatt) – for these are gods that cannot save because nothing we make ourselves is able to withstand the ravages of time.

Who could have predicted that the assassination of two obscure mid-European aristocrats in Sarajevo in 1914, and the defects of the Treaty of Versailles in 1919, would be the detonators of two wars that ravaged the entire globe? From the rubble, out of suffering beyond belief, has emerged the fragile skeleton of a new world order, but you would need the strong stomach of a Hebrew prophet to declare roundly that what was shaken needed to be.

I saw this stern lesson about the shaking out of both the good and the bad together at its most dramatic during the 1950s and 1960s when I spent almost 20 years in Central Africa during the freedom struggle, and watched societies shaken to their foundations both by constitutional change and by bloody revolution. And the poignancy of the moral was this. When the balance sheet of history is drawn up, it will, I believe, be seen that the British colonial system on balance did much more good than harm in Africa, in establishing systems of health and education and justice and laying the foundations of parliamentary democracy. But there came a point when it had to go, where it had reached a dead end, where it was frustrating the political and cultural and spiritual development of the peoples of Africa, where it was cramping their very souls. It had to be shaken out. And it was.

It takes tough-mindedness to trace divine purpose and meaning emerging from the degree of chaos and volume of human suffering I witnessed in Africa. The shaking out of colonialism was both inevitable and awful. But that wasn't the end of Africa's travails – even at the time, only the most purblind of secular optimists were predicting an unclouded future for the continent. The shaking has helped to forge a new Africa, but it is no Utopia, as a casual glance at any day's newspaper will reveal. It is those wheat and weeds again; wrapped round one another, totally intertwined.

Or take another example much nearer home. Has the Church escaped the shaking? Our doctrines, disciplines and discipleship have been put to the test of durability and truth in a Western society which neither persecutes nor indulges us but marginalizes us in the nicest possible way. And it is not just what was superficial or mistaken or faithless about our communal life that has been shaken out; many good people have been lost to the Church and important areas of witness have been wiped out.

The Western Church is undergoing a harrowing all right, but it is not unprecedented. Consider the shaking which the first generation of Christians endured, as in conditions of near chaos they awaited the imminent return of the Lord in glory. And when the Second Coming didn't come, what was there left for them to believe? The *parousia* – the Glorious Return of Christ – was the very linchpin of their faith, the light in which they viewed the entire gospel.

Could there be a more poignant theme than the struggle and anguish of the early Christians trying to readjust their time perspective as it began to dawn on them that rather than a sudden, joyous, supernatural climax to the Jesus-event, there lay ahead what turned out to be a long, hard slog?

That was a crisis unprecedented in Christian history, yet the Church survived that shaking, and became a much greater, more universal reality than if the original hope had been fulfilled to the letter. Christianity was transformed from an offshoot of a Jewish sect in a backwater of the Roman Empire to a great world religion. Yet even then, after surviving that shaking, its subsequent history has not been of a triumphal progression from glory to glory, but a strange, broken, episodic story of decay and renewal, sudden ends and strange new beginnings. One shaking follows another.

Now to what end is this sombre lesson; why is it that what can be shaken, ought to be? The Bible's explanation is that God wills a new creation which may be a gift from beyond history, the kingdom of heaven, but which is made up of elements from every era in history that have withstood the shaking, gone through the refiner's fire and had the dross burned off them. Nothing tawdry, second-rate, idolatrous about us or our society can stand in that latter day upon the earth when what has been hidden is revealed and in Paul's words, God is seen to be all in all (1 Corinthians 15.28). What can be shaken has got to be. Everything about the resplendent kingdom must be capable of bearing the intolerable weight of divine glory.

Secondly, perceive it is God who does the shaking.

'I will shake the heavens and the earth . . .' This is a central theme of the Old Testament, the idea of the dynamic God who is not only sovereign over history but actively at work in it, who not only reigns but rules, using who and what he chooses to accomplish his purposes. Go right back to Israel's search for nationhood. God addresses Moses, not from the remoteness of the heaven of heavens but out of a thicket. When Moses asks God his name, according to one translation he gets the enigmatic reply, 'Call me, "I will do what I will do."' This is a picturesque way of warning the Hebrew leader that God can only be known in history by his actions.

Indeed, so closely interwoven are God's being and his actions that it is only stretching grammar a little to suggest that God is not just a proper noun but also an active verb. We know God is around by the speed at which things change, and it is the speed at which God initiates change colliding with our resistance to change that creates turmoil. In fact, a good definition of a godless society is one which for all its technological virtuosity is static because no new human possibilities can break out of its inner deadness.

So God's people got on the move out of the secure serfdom of Pharaoh's kingdom into the deadly freedom of the uncharted desert. And whenever they got off course, God hauled them back with utter ruthlessness, not baulking, if the prophets are to be believed, at using war, captivity and pestilence as his instruments. People with a destiny have to be kept moving.

But the People of Israel lost their capacity or appetite for change. They sat at ease in Zion, building their great Temple, evolving all the impedimenta of organized religion. The grand sweep of the Law was splintered into 600 moralistic rules. The surge of power had gone; though they kept one ear cocked for the arrival of the Messiah, they lived according to the usages of their past.

As the Old Testament context of my text makes clear, just as God shook the moral order when he gave his chosen people the Law, so in the fullness of time, he shook that Law as he moved towards the final fulfilment of his will through Jesus, liberating new power out of the old religion. But those who hate change except on their own terms decided to stop it dead, so they took Jesus and put him in one place and nailed him down, to stop the shaking. In crucifying Jesus the powers that be imagined they were doing one thing; in fact they were being used to accomplish another. They became instruments of the God who shook the tomb until it fell apart and let loose his great agent of change into all the world and for all time.

The message (or is it an ultimatum?) is plain. God is shaking the structures of our society, using a motley crew of collaborators, revolutionaries and reformers, militants and atheists, to test whether they are flexible enough to aid humanity's movement towards a liberated, open future or a stubborn barrier against it. If we do not harmonize our discipleship with the rhythm of God's action we shall be swept aside, hindrances to the realization of the kingdom; creatures of the moment rather than citizens of the New Jerusalem.

Thirdly, cling to the things that have withstood the shaking.

I choose four New Testament affirmations about things that have withstood the shaking. The first is the consistent nature of God – Paul writing to Timothy, God 'remains faithful – for he cannot deny himself' (2 Timothy 2.13). This was one of the great discoveries in the history of religion; the reason why it is not hyperbole to describe the Jews as possessing religious genius. At a time when the peoples all round them were in thrall to gods noted for their capriciousness, the Jews discovered and then clung tenaciously to their belief in the moral consistency of Yahweh.

Recall Abraham pleading for the lives of the inhabitants of Sodom whom God had resolved to destroy because of their wickedness. Modestly and persistently the old patriarch got God to reduce his terms for a reprieve – suppose there are fifty righteous in the city, forty . . . ten? Then he makes his final appeal in an unanswerable argument – 'Shall not the Judge of all the earth do what is just?' (Genesis 18.25). In other words, there are certain things that not even God could do because they would violate his own nature.

The American preacher and novelist Lloyd C. Douglas is almost forgotten these days, but there is a revealing passage in his autobiography. When he was a university student, he had lodgings in a big house on the ground floor of which lived an old music teacher, housebound through infirmity. Douglas would call in on him every morning to see if he needed anything, popping his head round the door and asking the same ritual question, 'What's the good news today, sir?' And he'd get the same ritual answer. The old man would pick up a tuning fork and strike it on the table, 'Hear that?' he'd say. 'That's middle C; it was middle C yesterday and the day before. It will be middle C tomorrow and for a thousand years to come. Though the tenor across the hall sings flat and the piano upstairs is out of tune and there is noise, noise all round me, that, my friend, remains middle C.'

Middle C, a constant in the midst of turmoil and dissonance – consistency at the heart of the universe. And the author of the Letter to the Hebrews gave middle C a personal name. In a great leap of understanding, he cried, 'Jesus Christ is the same yesterday and today and for ever' (13.8). That is a note we have to strike when everything around us is out of tune.

The second affirmation, surprisingly, is about the Church; Jesus saying to his disciples, 'On this rock I will build my church, and the gates of Hades will not prevail against it' (Matthew 16.18). That takes some believing. It doesn't require a higher degree in Church history to think of periods when the Church has died, really and truly died, not merely sunk into a state of catalepsy like a sleeping princess awaiting the kiss of life from a princely lover. When the Roman Empire expired and the Dark Ages covered the earth, Church and state were so intertwined that it was taken for granted that when one went down the other went with it. Christianity had run its course. Yet when the curtain rose on the next act, the Middle Ages proper, there was Thomas Aquinas occupying the chair Aristotle had vacated, surrounded by eager young men who had travelled from all over Europe to sit at his feet and learn how to be priests.

In North Africa, not once but twice Islam put Christianity to the sword. And so on and on. Death, real death. The Church has died, and not always gloriously on a cross, but sometimes weak with old age and comfortably in its bed, and onlookers have seen the corpse laid to rest and gone away muttering, 'And we thought that you might have saved Israel.' Then has occurred an extraordinary thing. The community of faith has sprung into new life, presumably because it has a Lord who knows how to find his way out of a tomb.

Perhaps in our day, through those grim statistics of decline, God is challenging the Church in the West to start believing its own rhetoric. This is a classical preaching theme – the notion that like its Lord, the Church may have to suffer death in order to rise again to new life. We quote Jesus' words about the grain of wheat falling into the ground and dying in order to produce a harvest. Do Christians really believe that, or is the theme of death and resurrection merely a metaphor, a dramatic pictorial image of the ups and downs of the Western Church? Jesus' death was not metaphorical; it was actual, bloody, painful and final. If we do mean business when we preach and sing about the Church dying in order to rise again, then the key question we have to address is not, 'Have we faith that the Church will not die in spite of all the gloomy evidence to the contrary?' but, 'Dare we believe that if it does, it can rise again?'

I don't pretend to understand this strange phenomenon, the dying and rising Church. Just as Christ walked on water, so there have been times when it seems that the Christian faith has walked on air as the Church collapsed under it. This apparent defiance of the law of gravity is possible because in the time of the Church's shaking, the reality of the faith has been embodied in the secretly present kingdom, and it is a grave error to assume that the Church and kingdom are inextricably joined together like Siamese twins – that if one is sick, the other must be ailing.

Some of Jesus' most evocative images of the kingdom suggest that it is present in any age, anonymously and imperceptibly as salt giving tang to food, leaven fermenting dough, seed growing secretly. Each operates not by standing out from the surrounding mass and maintaining a separate identity, but by being swallowed up without trace in the whole substance.

God's aim is not to build stronger churches but to renew creation. Still, he has found it worthwhile to raise the Church from the dead on more than one occasion, and Jesus' words about the gates of hell not prevailing against it have thus far been fulfilled, because it is founded on the rock of countless confessions of Christ unto death, upon the rock of regenerate human nature and upon the rock of God's implacable purpose.

A third affirmation concerns the nature of personal obedience: Paul assuring the Christians at Corinth that when all else passes away, faith, hope and love abide. These are not random virtues; they are the essential dimensions of the Christian life, which is defective if it neglects any of the three. Hope is possible because the one who follows the way of Christ has faith that there is no human situation, however unpromising, which is impervious to love. Here are the three pillars on which the kingdom of God is raised in the life of the individual believer – faith venturing beyond the unprovable, love forgiving the unpardonable and hope remaining undimmed against all odds. And the character of personal discipleship is mirrored in the Christian community: faith defines the Church, love is its driving force and hope keeps it in existence.

But the crunch point comes when we face the ultimate challenge, the possibility of personal extinction. And this a final unshakeable affirmation: Jesus says, 'Because I live, you will live also.'

In the end it is not the clash of great forces, the rise and fall of empires, the vast sweeps of history that personally shake us most. In the universal scheme of things, we are mere ants crawling across a great canvas. It is that enemy, time, which shakes us most as it moves on, first at a creep and then at an accelerating pace towards who knows what fate? If the blank stare of the grave ends everything, then this Christian life may have been an adventure and a challenge and we may have done our bit for Christ and his kingdom, but what consolation is it if all things are to be made new, but we cannot share the joy and fulfilment of it?

In the end, the ultimate vindication of the gospel is not that it makes this world more endurable but that it makes another world real. Either Christianity is an enterprise of eternal significance or else it is nothing much. As Matthew Arnold said, 'No religion can long survive the decay of its belief in immortality; otherwise it becomes little more than morality touched with emotion.'

Yet there is no shaking so poignant or final as that which personally faces us in the inevitability of our mortality. It seems a tragic absurdity that billions of years of evolutionary pain should have gone into the making of a human being whose lifespan passes in the flicker of God's eye. This sense of outrage at the obliteration of any human being, great or humble, has from time immemorial given rise to the tenaciously held belief enshrined in many religions that physical death cannot be the end, that there must be some world, some unknown but real dimension of existence where the love, truth and joy which have enriched our lives through those we have loved and lost shine out in undimmed radiance. Plato based his entire argument for the immortality of the soul on the conviction that a world without his dead teacher and friend Socrates was unthinkable.

But it doesn't follow that something is true because we desperately want it to be so, though we do well to ponder Pascal's dictum that when God wants to make a point with his children, he plants it deeper than their minds, in their instincts. The Christian gospel's affirmation about the reality of eternal life avoids subjectivism by beginning at the other end – not in any convictions about the immortality of the soul but in a declaration about the nature of God. Taken at its most obvious, that sublime cliché, 'God is love' implies continuance of some sort, for love is the drive to unite all that is separated in time, space and condition. And in our brief time-span there are many forms of separation we cannot overcome. We shall meet our death as unfinished creatures, but because we have come to know the love of God, the infinite has been joined to the finite, the work of making us whole has begun and must persist until the enterprise is perfected.

But that is to make certain assumptions about the divine thought processes. And how is that possible? Well, we must appeal to the grand rule of theology – we must not deny to God any qualities we humans demonstrate at our highest and best. Now apply it to this question of eternal life. When we humans reflect on how this world appears to be with its finitude, its perishing, it is legitimate to ask: would we have created such a world in which the human spirit is intended to burn with a fierce bright flame for just a handful of years before flickering and vanishing? Would we have created a world which clings to the lowest, inanimate matter, and lets the highest, human personality, go? If the mountain outlasts the one who first climbed it; if Mozart's manuscripts are more enduring than the mind that conceived them; if the saint's mummified body is preserved but the soul aflame with God which occupied it is no more, then the universe is an affront to sanity, let alone morality. And if we would not create such a world, we need have no fear that God did.

And this instinct is given historical confirmation by the resurrection of Jesus not just as a sequel to the gospel or even as a climax to it but as the truth in whose light the Gospels came to be written at all. The whole point of the gospel message is that the purposes of God have been accomplished in the life, death and resurrection of Jesus. And since Jesus has conquered death, all those alive with his life have their deaths behind them in all but the biological sense. 'Because I live, you also will live,' says Jesus (John 14.19). Beyond the shaking.

Beyond the shaking. We cannot imagine what that new creation which emerges on the farther side of the final shaking will look like. Not even the most sanctified imagination can grapple with the consequences of the return of our Lord Jesus in glory. But we are assured there will be one familiar landmark in this new creation – the cross, for as the Book of Revelation declares, in what has to be one of the most powerful metaphors in all Scripture, a bleeding lamb has been sitting on the throne of the universe from the beginning; God not in his judgemental but in his redemptive role.

What can we know about the great sweep of God's providence? We tie ourselves hopelessly in knots trying to theologize about it. Our rhetoric peters out for lack of an adequate vocabulary by which to describe this great mystery. But sometimes, what we cannot say we can sing. In the echo-chamber of my memory, from the Methodist chapel of my childhood, I can still hear a Victorian gospel chorus which from the superior heights of my theological education I came to regard pityingly as spiritually simplistic and poetically banal. Yet it puts into one phrase, one vivid image, the nub of the issue. 'I will cling to the old rugged cross.' Clinging to the old rugged cross – that's the only secure place to be when the heavens and earth are shaken to their foundations.